The Well
and
The Woman

Positioning Yourself
For
Destiny

Margaret Peat

The Well and The Woman

ISBN: 978-1-907929-87-8

You can contact Margaret at: KMPeat@aol.com

lp

Editing, design and layout by Life Publications
www.lifepublications.org.uk

Dedication

To the special people who have taught me that everyone has a story...

Acknowledgements

Kevin Peat...thank you for your support, patience, ideas and creativity which add greatly to this book. You are forever my inspiration in life...

Jan and David Holdaway...thank you for your guidance, patience and expertise in making this book happen. You are so much appreciated.

Commendations

Every book Margaret has written has brought blessing, challenge, and change into the lives of those who have read them (myself included.) This book will be used by God to "bring its readers to the place where their destiny can become a reality." I love the quote, one amongst many, "The water of the River of Life flowing inside of you is the most important thing you have. Let it flow!" This book contains life changing truths and will, I believe, bring transformation to many.

Ray Jones
Minister and Author

After reading *The Well and the Woman*, you will never again read the Bible story of the Samaritan woman's encounter with Jesus the same way. Margaret weaves in a myriad of enriching cultural details which bring this story and its truths even more to life. She doesn't stop there, however, but distills the essential questions from the story and invites us to personalize them. Margaret's story goes from 'The Story', to 'Our Story' even to 'Our God Story'. You will be challenged and enriched by this book.

Betsy Kylstra
Co-Founder of Restoring The Foundations

This book is a good read for individuals and groups who want to encounter the heart of God. Margaret's writing is refreshingly open and engaging, leading the reader into a deeper awareness and experience of God. As Margaret shares stories of life alongside the biblical story of *The Woman at the*

Well, God's heart is made accessible to those who are searching for meaning, deeper relationship and to realise their destiny in God's purposes.

Michelle Nunn
Senior Pastor of Nantwich Elim Church

In this captivating book Margaret takes us behind the story to glimpse the imagined circumstances and events that surround the story of Jesus' encounter with the Samaritan woman at the well. Drawing on her fruitful years of ministry, she shares many insightful, helpful and inspiring thoughts. An excellent collection of literary jewels making for an edifying and enjoyable devotional treasure.

David Campbell, Regional Leader
Metropolitan East and West Regions
Elim Pentecostal Church

This book is amazing! Margaret has used great insight in telling the unexpected, a very special conversation of a woman with Jesus and His response to her and her people.
The devotional chapters are full of meaningful and inspirational thoughts that challenge the reader and we highly recommend this book.

This is a masterful follow on from Margaret's previous seven books and will inspire readers with their own heart response to the insightful stories she tells. It is also a great tool for small groups of people to use as a devotional study together.

Bob and Maggie Lawson
Former General Superintendent of Elim Churches
in New Zealand

Contents

The Well and The Woman

Foreword

Kevin and Margaret Peat have been among our closest friends for very many years. Yet there were two more pressings reasons why I responded so positively and warmly to the invitation to write a Foreword for this book.

The first was the awareness that Margaret Peat has over recent years become a prolific author whose books – written with warmth, humour, sensitivity and insight – have touched the lives of so many people, and having seen this latest manuscript I recognised that this was most certainly not going to be an exception.

The other reason was the subject matter itself. Kevin and Margaret have always worked very closely together in ministry over the years and I can remember introducing Kevin to a group of leaders on one occasion as 'An apostle of the heart'. By that I meant that he and Margaret understand the powerful and significant command in Proverbs 4:23 to *"Above all else guard your heart for everything you do springs from it."* I have watched them faithfully teach this, and I have watched them live by it.

The heart is so often seen in scripture as an underground spring – a well.

The moment I saw the title of this book my mind leapt immediately to the story of *The Keeper of the Spring*. It tells of an old man who lived in the hills that surrounded a picturesque beauty spot that attracted multitudes of visitors. The focal point was a small lake that teemed with birds and wildlife. His job was simple – to maintain the springs in the surrounding hills that fed into the lake. He rarely came down to the town and, few people ever saw him.

In a cost-cutting exercise the local council decided to dispense with his services. For a while very little changed but over a period of time the small lake became polluted and the waters increasingly toxic. Before long the wildlife left and with them the tourists. The council was to learn the lesson that their area's greatest resource had been the purity of the source.

One of my favourite verses in the Old Testament is Genesis 49:22, KJV, *"Joseph is a fruitful bough, by a well; whose branches run over the wall"*. It reveals that when there is wellness in the well fruitfulness is guaranteed and no barriers or walls can contain the power of what ensues.

This is why what you are about to engage with in this insightful book is so relevant, and more importantly, vital to your growth and spiritual success – enjoy.

John Glass
General Superintendent, Elim Churches (2000-2016)
Chair of Council, Evangelical Alliance (2014-2018)

Preface

I have always enjoyed a good story and when I read the true stories of the Bible, I am always wondering more about who and how, what and where? There are thousands of little details behind every Bible story which we will never know but which really happened.

We read hundreds of real life stories in our Bible and some of them are just a couple of sentences long. But hidden within the lines of each, however long or short, are a whole host of events and actions and feelings, hopes and disappointments and dreams fulfilled that we will never know. And they really happened too.

Here in this book, I have taken the story of the woman at the well and woven around her a story which may or may not have happened and have used this as a launchpad to share nine devotional chapters based on this important event recorded in John 4.

What an absolute date with destiny! A woman who was a failure in the eyes of the world...touched by God in human form and suddenly her destiny becomes a reality. And yours can too. She had no idea that she was positioning herself for destiny and often, neither do we. But there are things in our lives that can be honed, addressed or fine-tuned which put us in a place to be ready for His destiny to unfold.

I hope that through her story, and these simple thoughts that God Himself will touch your life again and your dreams of destiny will come true.

Margaret

Introduction

Last year, my husband Kevin and I went to Wimbledon. Beforehand I was incredibly excited and spent weeks planning everything and making a list of what I would need, sun hat, sunglasses, umbrella etc. Eventually the day arrived and we caught a flight, and set off to the ground in plenty of time. I had researched the Tube journeys and had a piece of paper with everything carefully written down.

We caught the Tube and headed for the *All England Tennis Club*. We had our tickets safely in our bag and everything we would need and we counted the stops to the ground. At last we came to Wimbledon Tube Station, got off the train and began to follow the thousands of people towards the ground.

On the way we decided to buy some juice and sweets for the day and it was while we were standing by the Pepsi Max that I said to Kevin,

"Where's the bag with the tickets and things in?"

"You've got the bag," he said.

"No, you've got the bag."

"No...you had the bag!"

Suddenly we realised that we were standing in a shop and our treasured tickets were in a bag on the train, travelling up by themselves to the end of the line!

I cannot tell you how fast we raced back against the flow of thousands of people to the Tube station. I was more scared of my Auntie who had bought us those tickets than of missing the match and I was wondering, should I break the news that we had lost the tickets or sit and watch the match on TV, research every aspect of Wimbledon and describe what a wonderful day we'd had?

To cut a very long story short, when someone leaves an unattended bag on the Tube, no one steals it because no one wants to go near it for fear of it being something dangerous! So our precious bag travelled in a very big space of its own to the end of the line where it was examined then put in lost property, and we arrived on the next train to claim it back! We needed those tickets for the match.

Do you have your ticket for this moment with God? A sense of anticipation that He might have something to say to you? Or did you lose it earlier today or yesterday? Did something happen and you picked up that issue and left your ticket on the seat?

God has given you an individually designed ticket of anticipation for what is in store. Do you have it here? Sometimes distractions at home, at work or with family cause you to let go of your ticket for a 'God designed moment'. You read or you listen or you discuss but your mind is somewhere else? You've lost your ticket!

When you picked up this book, you picked up an invisible ticket too, and that ticket is for you now. It belongs to nobody else and He has something special to say to you today.

Get ready!

The Story of the Woman at the Well

I couldn't believe he was dead! I stared at Galiano speechless on that day he told us all those years ago. I was utterly lost for words as he described the events he had witnessed. I've remembered his words for over twenty years and they are still as fresh to me today as then...

"I was sewing the last few stitches to the sandals I was making," he described, breaking his small loaf into two and helping himself to more olives, *"when I looked outside and saw the sky looked just like night. Well it disturbed me and I stopped stitching and went outside. There were neighbours in the street, also looking around and I remember they were pointing at something in the sky. Eventually I went back in and continued sewing and my wife began preparation for our evening meal. Suddenly, everything began to shake – a little at first then more and more. I remember the oil lamp fell and the oil spilled on the floor..."*

I sat transfixed as Galiano told me about that earthquake and the rocks that split into pieces. My mind was racing.

The Well and The Woman

"There were all sorts of strange and wonderful happenings everywhere..." He paused for a moment, as though he were right there in that moment once again.

"One family in our village had just finished the week of funeral rituals for their mother and suddenly, she was right there with them again. Very much alive! There were reports all over the city, of similar things. Deceased brothers, wives, fathers and children being seen in the city, not by one or two but by many, many people."

I sat quietly as Galiano had explained these strange and wonderful things. He continued almost as though I were not with him.

"I decided to walk the ten miles to the city," he continued, *"to see what was happening there, and even a long way off I could hear the shouts and sounds of confusion. When I arrived at the temple I could not believe my eyes. There I saw what seemed like thousands of people around it. Some spoke of ghosts, some of the fall of the altar but when I finally found out the truth from the rumours, I discovered that at the time of the earthquake, the curtain of the temple had ripped top to bottom and was now in two parts. No one near, it just happened. Just like the earthquake. Just like the darkness and just like the splitting of the rocks!"*

I stared at him that day, trying to take it in as he told me of the three crosses and the sign above one of them which read *Jesus of Nazareth, King of the Jews.* I imagined it in my mind's eye. My spirit was heavy. My mind was confused at that moment as I thought back to my own life changing event. Also long ago, yet I remember it as yesterday...

....

The Story of the Woman at the Well

I'd always longed for something really special to happen. I was born in the little village where I've lived my whole life in a house made with straw and clay bricks.

The first thing I remember is watching my mother sweep the clay floor of our little home. We lived in this one room which was divided so that our sheep and goats could live in the other end in winter. One of the parts was raised and that's where we slept. The lower part had a fire for heating and cooking and we would keep the fire going by collecting sticks, dried grass, charcoal and animal dung. We played games there and my mother would weave and sew. There was just one small, high window and the walls had lots of crevices and niches into which were placed bowls, food and clothes and anything we needed to store. It was dark inside, even on a sunny day so I spent most of my time outdoors.

My mother's life was centred around our home and all her time was taken up with looking after us children, cleaning the home and cooking for our family and any guests who might turn up at the door. Mother loved having guests.

In preparation, we would make a visit to the market to buy what she needed for the meal and then, with me at her side, she would clean through the house and then begin to make the meal. Flour was ground between two stones and the dough was mixed and kneaded and then the round loaves were placed onto the open fire. Fresh loaves had to be baked every other day but when guests were due, special ones were made and the flour was mixed with mint or herbs or even locusts. They were my favourites. Locusts were the visitors' special treat. We never had locusts ourselves. We would just dry them in the sun, grind them to powder and mix them with flour or honey and bake them on the fire. That was the nearest I got to a locust meal! Sometimes honey doughnuts were fried in a pan too.

The Well and The Woman

Once the visitor arrived, and had removed his shoes, it was my job to give him a drink of water. Mother would pour water over his feet, rub them with her hands and then dry them with a cloth. Then we would sit down to eat dinner and hands were washed and a prayer would be offered for the meal. Mother would have placed the big pot of food on a mat on the floor and we sat cross legged around it.

Dinner usually included vegetables, lentils, cucumbers and onions made up into a stew and we used bread to scoop up the vegetables and soak up the juice. Sometimes my father and the visitor would have a small fish or tiny piece of meat but there was never any for mother or my brother and I. Once that was eaten we always ended our meals with fruit and the washing of hands once more.

Our food was seasoned with herbs or mustard and on one occasion we sat down to eat as a family and someone had put double the mustard in the food. No one knew who had done it though my brother looked very guilty! My father was furious and we were both punished. I was made to do double cleaning and my brother, double school work for a whole month.

There was always local wine with our food and when guests came, often my father would sit with them drinking until very late. I could hear them laughing and talking as they sat outside the house in the warm evening air, telling stories. It was an insult to leave early so visitors always stayed till late. Eventually my mother would lie down beside me and later, my father also after he had secured the door with a wooden bar to keep us safe. We covered ourselves with a goat's hair blanket but my tunic, and the heat of the others kept me nice and warm.

Some people had an upper room but we just had a roof. In hot weather, we would drag the straw mattress up the stairs at the side of the house and sleep on the roof. There was a parapet round the edge for safety as the roof was also used to pray, for storage and to see a long way! That's where we also dried the grain, fruits and locusts too.

The houses were joined together so we could run from roof to roof and often did, until some adult called us down. Most houses were built together for security and isolated houses were uncommon in our town. Hopscotch, ball games and marbles were popular and throwing stones into a pit and weddings and funerals too.

I grew up learning from my mother. She was a wise woman. "Face your fears..." she would say to me. "Don't run away. Stand up and face those problems." She said many things that would help me in the life I would live. She taught me many useful skills too; baking, weaving and spinning in addition to domestic duties, but I was always wishing I could go to learn with my brother. I would try to listen as he was taught to read and write by my father and try to recite the numbers I heard as I kneaded the dough for our bread.

Our neighbour, Salem, was very kind and sometimes he would pretend to not notice as I crept into his house and listened to him teaching his son from the five books of the Law. He would tell him stories of how Moses received the Law and I would listen in awe and wonder of our forefathers of long ago and how God led them and blessed them. I learned the names of the five books of the law and could say them by heart, and my brother and I would swap stories as we lay on our mattress at night in the shadow of the oil lamp. Salem would always take his son to the corner of the room at the end of the lesson giving me the chance to escape back into the bright sunlight.

All my education was provided by my mother and as I got older, it was my job to fetch the water from the well, wash our clothes in the stream and go to the market at the start or end of each day. From the age of three years old, my brother began to get religious education and then in time, he began to learn a trade but I continued to be educated only in domestic duties. I was allowed to ask questions about festivals as they occurred but that was the extent of my religious instruction from my parents.

One day I heard a terrible wailing coming from next door and Mrs Salem ran screaming from the house. My mother disappeared for a while leaving me alone and a short time later the screaming stopped. Soon after she took me round to Salem's but instead of sitting at the table where he always sat teaching his son, he was lying still, eyes closed. I watched as Mother washed him and wrapped him in linen. Their family was gathering for weeping and many wore sackcloth or torn clothes. We placed myrrh and aloes between the linen and I felt so sad as I saw him there. Sad for Mrs Salem and her son. Sad for Salem for he was a kind man. But most of all sad that I could no longer creep to my favourite corner and learn of God from this wise man.

I no longer had stories to trade with my brother at night before we slept but he would often still tell me what he had learned that day. One night he told me that our little village in Samaria was once a great city. That on the mountain which overlooks our house was built a magnificent temple which rivalled the one in Jerusalem. But one day it was destroyed, my brother said, and it lay in ruins even though it had been our place of worship for many years. I had often wondered why we worshipped God on that mountain.

My brother told me lots more through the weeks and months that followed Salem's death, almost as though he wanted to make up for my sadness. Then one day, my education stopped abruptly!

....

The Story of the Woman at the Well

I was thirteen years old when my parents sat me down and explained to me that I was going to be married.

"Married?" I thought. "I'm only a child." But I knew that many young girls were promised in marriage at my age. I was miserable and afraid but I knew that I could not refuse. I didn't want to leave my parents and my brother and go to join another man's family but I knew that's how it had to be. I so envied my brother who, being a boy would stay with our family and one day bring a wife back to become part of my home. It was already arranged my parents said. They had made a legal promise and our betrothal would be exactly one year. The next day I met my future husband. His name was Janos. It means 'God is merciful' and in time, I would discover that God was indeed merciful in bringing to me this husband.

Janos and I were not allowed to be alone and I often wished I had the opportunity to get to know him better. To begin with, I would cry myself to sleep but as time went by and our wedding week of celebrations were planned, musicians were booked and guests were notified, I began to warm to the idea of becoming someone's wife. My family prepared for the wedding and my future husband prepared what would be our home within his own family home.

The wedding day arrived and I was dressed in a beautiful dress and felt like a queen. It was as if we were King and Queen for the day! I was covered by a veil which hid me from sight and later that day as the veil was lifted, and I set eyes on my new husband, I knew I would love him and he would love me too. There was much music and dancing as we celebrated the beginning of this new chapter of life together. I can still hear those harps, tambourines and pipers to this day...

We settled into life in his family home and made it our home. We planted our own olive tree which would thrive and grow through the years as we served our God together. I knew from my visits to the well listening to the other girls talk, how blessed I was.

"I'd be better sold as a slave," said one, on one occasion.

"At least in seven years you'd be free," replied the other.

But we were happy and we were blessed.

It was two years later when I heard someone shouting as they ran breathless into the village. I caught only three words. "Janos! Accident! Dead!"

And so my life changed once again. Janos was gone. A week of mourning at our home took place and I was now a widow at sixteen years old.

....

I walked barefoot for weeks as is the custom of a grieving widow in our land. But if my feet were sore, my heart was more so. I wanted Janos so much. To see his smile, to hear his voice, to feel his touch. I needed him – as my provider, as my protector, as my reason to exist.

But slowly and surely, day by day, week by week, the love and care of Janos' family wrapped around me and I began to gradually live again. Janos' father, Asher, was a great help to me, a widower himself, knowing my needs at each stage of grief. When he told me that he would himself give me food and shelter and take me as his wife, I cried, suddenly free from the heavy burden of finding a man who would provide these things. I knew, if I wasn't forced by social pressure to marry, then I would be forced by economic need and this to me was a much better option.

Asher reminded me so much of Janos and I felt safe and secure in his family. I cared for him as best I could. That was my wifely duty after all – to look after my husband. Even though only sixteen years old, I dressed older than my years, my long hair, which had never been cut, was braided and tied up by day and covered with my veil when I left the house.

I would daily visit the village well, clean the house and then pick fruit and vegetables from the garden for our meal. We would regularly take produce to the market to sell. The market was a busy and cheerful place but Asher's real love was his garden. What wonderful sights, sounds and scents hit us each time we spent time there. Asher spent hours there – a living treasure trove built up throughout the years of his life. Fig and date palms, almond trees and grape vines. Asher's garden brought both him and I so much pleasure in the time we spent together. I would pick and chop the onions and lentils, garlic and leeks, season them with herbs and bake them on the fire. We would sit and eat under the stars talking of Janos and laughing over the little things he did.

Sometimes Asher's friends visited. There was one particular man who came a lot called Jacob. Jacob was tall and handsome and a real gentleman. Dressed in a long tunic, leather sandals and gold rings on his right hand, his presence always seemed to fill the room. On one occasion, my husband and he talked and I cooked many different types of vegetables fried in olive oil and roasted meat on the open fire. I served them and then continued working by the outside fire while they ate and drank and sat together through the evening.

Jacob was obviously a rich man by what he spoke of and by how he dressed, but he seemed comfortable with my husband and there was always much talking and laughing when he came to visit.

I was still clearing away outside and preparing a few things for the next day's meal when Jacob left. Suddenly, I heard a noise and there was Jacob right behind me. I spun round startled and looked up at him. He was coming slowly towards me. And then I saw his eyes and I was shocked! Eyes full of passion and desire. I backed off afraid, dropping a clay dish in my haste. The dish smashed and as the noise echoed in the stillness of the evening, Asher called my name from within the house. It was the most wonderful sound I had ever heard and I fled indoors. I said nothing as I prepared for bed but I lay awake for many hours with those eyes imprinted on my mind!

Weeks turned into months and months into years and as Asher grew older, I would tenderly wash his face and his feet, help dress him and assist him as he walked out in the noonday sun. Even though I was only a woman, he always seemed proud to have me by his side.

One day, however, he did not rise, he did not call me to his side and his eyes did not light up as they met mine. I stood by his bed for a while, closed my eyes and let the peace of the moment engulf me. In that moment, I knew I was alone again.

....

I married Jacob in the spring. I knew I would be the second wife in the home but it solved my immediate dilemma of finding food, shelter and finance. Besides, to begin with everything was fine. I had robes specially made for me and a long embroidered tunic with a wide sash. I wore gold earrings and bracelets and ankle rings too. I even had makeup to wear when guests came around. Jacob was obviously a wealthy man and there was plenty of money to spare. My own personal space had comfortable furniture and a proper bed of wood. I loved snuggling down under the fine wool blankets and pillows. The food was very good and we ate meat, cheese and eggs regularly.

The Story of the Woman at the Well

It seemed that Jacob and his wife had everything they wanted. That was except for one thing. They were childless and longed for a baby – sons and heirs – children to care for them in their old age. And I discovered that's where I came in! But as the weeks and months passed and no baby arrived for them through me, their generosity and kindness subsided. His wife seemed to resent my presence so much and within a year Jacob too, was treating me with contempt. I had increasingly become their slave, doing nothing more than serving their every whim.

And then the beatings began. The first time was when I dropped a plate of food in the courtyard and the second, because Jacob felt that I was too visible when they were entertaining a visitor. Then I was often shut in a room for hours on end with no food or water until eventually my life was so miserable I wished I could die.

One day Jacob handed me a written bill, letting me know of our divorce and I packed my belongings and changed into the clothes I arrived in. I left without money, I had no change of clothes and I had nowhere to go.

My parents by this time were both dead and my brother was far away. Where could I go? What could I do? I ate scraps I found along the roadside and slept wherever I could. I would search through the pebble streets for any coins that had been lost.

At night in the dark streets, I would longingly watch the torches of fire light up the homes, which showed that sleepers were present and I would imagine them safe in their beds. I made my way to any fire which had been kept burning, for warmth and settled there to sleep for the night whenever I could. People went to bed early and the evenings were so long and it was always a relief when before dawn, people once again began on their daily business.

The Well and The Woman

People always got up early when there was more light and less heat. With only one room in most houses, it was difficult to stay in bed anyway. The men went to work as potters, carpenters, tentmakers or whatever their trade was. The older boys would go with them while the women and girls and younger boys did the household chores before the noonday sun made it too hot to work. The heat of the day was worse than the cold of the night and one day I was making my way to the well, so hungry, so thirsty when everything went black...

....

It must have been a few moments before I came to and someone was wiping my face with clear cool water. I raised my head and she put a vessel to my lips for me to drink from. The water tasted wonderful, cold and refreshing in my parched mouth. Her name was Joanna and she had found me as she came home from the well. Joanna let me sit a while till I felt better and then helped me to a nearby house – the home of her two brothers.

"I mustn't be away long," she said. "I am a servant at a house nearby but I could not leave you lying alone on the path to the well."

Soon Joanna left me and by nightfall it was settled. If I cooked, cleaned and looked after them both, then the eldest brother would make me his wife. I thought about it briefly. My choice was very limited. As a woman, I had inherited nothing from my three marriages and had no financial support whatsoever.

I considered my options. I could be a beggar. I could be a prostitute or I could be a wife to Thomas. I chose the latter.

In addition to buying the food daily, tidying and sweeping the floor, washing and cooking and keeping the fire going, I would make garments and sell them to the merchants working with wool and flax. I would spend the hours making blankets and tunics. I was able to help the poor and needy and often Thomas would bring a poor soul to our door.

One day Thomas drank some water that was not clean. He became very sick, had severe pain and a high fever. I did everything I could but he died within a few days. And so I stayed at that house and became the reluctant wife of his brother.

From the moment his brother died of dysentery, Samuel refused to drink any water. A heavy drinker of wine before his loss, over a period of time he began to consume gallons of alcohol and eventually drank from morning until night. His alcoholism was followed with physical abuse and at times I feared for my life. Many a time I would arrive at the well with bruises on my face hidden from view by my veil. Then he began to accuse me of going with other men. My daily visit to the well and to the market was the only time I was out of the house, but he became obsessed with this for months.

I looked forward to those daily trips and my eyes feasted on the multi coloured wild flowers on the wayside. God's creation never failed to give me the strength to go on. Then he began to follow me to the well and back. He kept well behind but I knew he was there.

I became used to the violence and would almost daily be pouring wine and olive oil onto my wounds to cleanse them and relieve my pain.

One day he came to me and knocked the bowl of oil and wine from my hand. It crashed onto the floor. I ran to the door very afraid.

"It's your fault!" he screamed at me. "You killed my brother with that water." I stared at him, unbelieving.

"Get out!" he screamed even louder, "and don't come back. If you ever come back, I will kill you!"

His words resounded in my head for many months. As I travelled past the huge oak trees, poplars, pines and firs, walking in the fields, watching wolves prey on sheep in the darkness of the night, those four words preyed on my mind. When walking through the thistles and thorns, watching foxes playing in the vines and seeing snakes and scorpions at the edge of the desert those words embroidered each scene. This was even worse than receiving a note of divorce. I actually wanted him to divorce me. I was imprisoned, unable to go forward but also not daring to go back.

I walked miles. The roads were bad and accommodation was rare even though I had a little money. Most people sleep in tents on long journeys but in the mild climate sleeping outdoors was no problem. Much of life is lived outside and on hot nights, many sleep in the open air.

I was on my way to Jerusalem, although I had no idea why, and the terrain was dry and the sun was hot. Journeys take weeks sometimes as it is the custom for travellers to stop and bring salutations whenever they meet other travellers.

It was dangerous for me to travel and bandits were a continual hazard. Men usually didn't travel alone, let alone women and there were several times I hid behind rocks or in caves, clutching my provisions as the travellers passed by. Most travelled early morning and in the evening when it was cooler so I didn't see many other people.

It was on the third day when I stopped that I turned behind me and stared at the long winding track. There was no road ahead, just a bumpy wide track where the stones had been cleared and many feet of people and animals had passed that way. I turned and gazed ahead as far as I could see. I watched a pack of dogs running from the direction of the town.

"What am I doing?" I said to myself. "Where am I going?"

I had answers to neither question. Then I heard a voice. It was my mother's voice all those years ago.

"You have to face your fears," she had said. "With the help of God, go back and face those problems."

I knew what I had to do. So picking up my pitcher of water and my small loaf of bread, I stood for a moment then began to walk back to the place of my birth.

....

By the time I got back to Sychar, I was almost out of provisions and knew that my money would run out soon. I found a job on a farm picking olives and figs. The farmer was kind – a widower – and often gave myself and the other girls some of what we had picked for him. To begin with I used to secretly sleep in his barns but one night I saw a wolf stealing his sheep and ran to his door banging loudly to wake him.

"What are you doing here so late at night?" he asked me once the crisis was resolved and the sheep were safely at peace once again.

I told him the whole story that night – all about my first love, Janos, and then his father Asher. I talked about my time with Jacob and how Joanna found me and took me to the home of her brothers. I told him of the beatings and how Samuel told me if I came back he would kill me. How could I still be married to such a wicked man? I asked myself out loud. I couldn't go back but I couldn't go on ahead. The farmer was called Peter and he invited me into his house.

"To everyone else, you are sleeping in my barn," he said, as he closed the door behind me...

And so my life continued. I would leave with the other women at the end of the day and later he would let me into the house. But soon everyone knew I was living with Peter. Life became very busy. The farm took a lot of time and each month held new challenges. Every January we would plant the vegetables which were watered by the late rain in March. March to October was our long hot summer and this was broken by the early rains in October and November. Many crops were harvested. In March and April we would gather the flax and in May and June the wheat and barley. July and August we would prune the vines and in August and September harvest the grapes, pomegranates and figs. I learned to take milk from the sheep and goats and make yoghurt, butter and cheese, to make clothes with the sheep's wool, and sew containers from goat skin.

The seasons came and went but life was settled. I had experienced so many changes in my life and I cared not, if nothing ever changed again. But there was to come a change that would turn my world around and the world of everyone around me. And that change was very close.

....

It was eleven in the morning and I had been up very early in the fields for it was to be a hot day. I had spent the morning sweeping the yard and then making goat skin containers for the new wine. I had been longer than I expected and as I looked at the sun, I realised it was near noon and I still hadn't fetched the daily supply of water. I preferred to go then anyway to avoid the looks of accusation which often followed me to the well and back. Lifting a water pot I set it comfortably on my hip and left the house for the well. It was a twenty minute walk and it was hot and dusty along the road.

I had been to Jacob's well many times through my lifetime. We called it Jacob's well as it was near to the ground Jacob gave to his son Joseph. I learned of it from our kind neighbour Salem many years ago. I couldn't see the well from afar as it was so dusty, but as I came nearer I could see quite clearly a figure by the side of the well. I stopped and peered into the dust. Was it a man? A man wouldn't be there at this time of day. Was it a woman? A woman wouldn't be sitting down, she would be hauling up the water to fill her water pots and then hurrying away to more tasks. Puzzled, I began to walk nearer, staring intently in front of me. After a few more steps I could see the outline of a man and I immediately felt wary. It could be anyone and there seemed to be no one else around. But I needed the water and I had no choice but to continue on, to where the man was sitting.

As I reached the well, I realised the man was a Jew. I could tell immediately by his clothes and when he spoke there was no doubt from his Galilean accent, he was indeed a Jew. What was a man doing here? That was strange. But a Jewish man? I reached the well and ignoring him, I began to lower the pitcher down into the well. Then he spoke.

"Would you give me a drink?" he asked.

I turned. He was looking straight at me. Now I was really confused. This man should not be speaking to me, a woman. This Jew should not be addressing me, a Samaritan. Why was this? So I asked him.

"How come you a Jew and a man are asking me, a Samaritan and a woman for a drink?"

The Well and The Woman

And then he spoke some more.

"If you knew who I am," he said to me "and who is asking you for a drink then it would be you asking me for a drink instead." I looked at him, confused. Who was he?

"I would give you living water," he added. I looked at him frowning.

"But you've no bucket to get me water." I replied cautiously. "And this is a deep well – you can't get the water."

The man smiled.

"How would you get the water?" I continued. "Are you greater than Jacob and his family who made the well to begin with?"

"Ah," said the man. "Those who drink from this well will get thirsty again."

He paused as I gazed at him, allowing his words to sink in. His eyes seemed to pierce my soul. There was a warmth in his manner. A kindness in his voice and a depth of love in his eyes, not a sexual love that I had seen so many times before, but an empathy, an unconditional, caring sort of love which made me want to continue this conversation. He carried on speaking.

"Yes, this water will only last for a while but anyone who drinks the water that I supply will never be thirsty again. Ever..." I looked around for a container where he could be storing this water but saw none. *"It must be back in Jerusalem,"* I thought.

"You see the water that I would give you would become a well of water, continually springing up inside you, giving you eternal life."

"Eternal life..." I repeated to myself. What wonderful words! I let the words meander through my mind and roll off my tongue silently. I didn't understand them but they did something in my heart every time I said them.

"Eternal life... Eternal life..." I repeated to myself. I imagined myself repeating them as I swept the yard, picked the grapes, crushed the olives.

"Eternal life... eternal life..." When people snubbed me in the shops because Peter wasn't my husband.

"Eternal life... Eternal life..."

"Give me this water..." I heard myself saying, "so I'm never thirsty again. Then I will never have to come down to this well again," I added, remembering the hundreds of heavy trips I had made in all seasons and conditions throughout my lifetime.

There was a silence for a moment or two while the man looked at me. His eyes were hard to read. Was it compassion? Puzzlement? Concern? He seemed to be looking right inside me. And then he seemed to make a decision.

"Go home, call your husband and then come back again." I stared at him doubtfully, then anxiously, then shamefully.

"I have no husband..." I replied softly, biting my bottom lip. My eyes were staring down into the dust beneath our feet.

"That's good you have told me the truth. You indeed have no husband. You have had five husbands and the man that you now have is not your husband." I looked up, eyes wide, my mouth dropping open. My mind was a whirl. Who was this stranger with eyes that burned my soul? Where did he come from? How did he know all about my life? And yet as he looked at me, there was no judgement in his face.

"Eternal life," I mused. "Eternal..." Could it be that he was a prophet? That would explain his amazing knowledge, his piercing words, his overwhelming presence...? A prophet! I seized the opportunity to question him further.

"Sir, I see you are a prophet? Well our fathers worshipped here on Mount Gerazim but you say that we should worship in Jerusalem?" I sat down now on the stone opposite him. He paused for a moment.

"Lady, there will come a time when we will worship God at neither Mount Gerazim or in Jerusalem. The thing is you see, you Samaritans worship what you don't know. We Jews know who we worship and the salvation of God is available through the Jews." I said nothing, but listened. Those two words were still pulsating round my mind.

"Eternal life," I mouthed silently.

"I tell you," he continued with passion. "There will come a day when real worshippers will worship the Father in spirit and in truth. In fact as God is spirit, that's how they must worship him. That's exactly who the Father seeks."

My mind was full of so many things – things that I'd never heard before and there was this eternal life thing which made me feel all strange and wonderful all at once! I shook my head wistfully.

"Well, all I know is that the Messiah IS coming and HE will tell us ALL things."

The man was standing now, and the words he spoke then raced through my mind and hit my heart like nothing had ever done before. He looked straight into my eyes and deep into my soul.

"I...AM HE!"

It was like the highest of highs and the lowest of lows. It was like a thousand memories flew through my mind in a second. It was like swimming in the deepest sea and flying on the wings of an eagle to the highest heights all at one time. I gazed at him and he at me and I wanted that moment to last forever...

"...Jeeeeesuuuuuus!"

A voice suddenly broke the moment. A man's voice from afar shouting.

"Jesus, we have food from the villaaaage..." and behind the man came other men, bearded, tanned, hot, breathless as they hurried up to where we stood.

Suddenly they saw me! The men stopped dead – and stared. There was silence as I stood before them. The look on their faces said everything. I just turned and ran as fast as I could, in my haste, leaving my water pot behind...

....

I remember it all as though it were yesterday. I ran as fast as I could back to the village, my heart beating. There was something about me that felt different. Was it a lightness in my spirit or a love in my heart? I don't know, but at that moment I knew that there, beside the well on that hot dusty day long ago, something had changed.

Reaching the village I looked left, then right for anyone I could see. There was a group of women outside a house and I ran to them.

"Come and see a man who has just told me my life story!" I said excitedly. "I believe he could be the Messiah!" I could hardly contain my excitement.

They looked at me, then chattering excitedly themselves began to hurry, then run down the pebble street towards Jacob's well. I could hear them shouting to others on the way as I went to various places in the village and told them what I believed – that I had met the Messiah at the well of Jacob!! Before long, many people, men, women and children were making their way on their journey of a lifetime.

Jesus and his friends were still at the well when we arrived. We listened to him talk to us and suddenly...everything made sense. We were receiving this 'living water' that he had spoken about and it was becoming a well deep down inside our very being!

I knew at that moment for myself and those around me that I would indeed never be thirsty again for that well would flow until the day I died.

Before I knew it the elders of the village had asked Jesus to stay for the night in the village and as Jesus, followed by crowds of people, made his way back into our village, I could hardly believe my eyes. A Jew staying at a Samaritan home in a Samaritan village? Unheard of!

Jesus stayed with us for two whole days never once wasting a minute, teaching us and sharing the good news with everyone who came. Many more people believed in him during those days.

"I'm so glad he came," said a woman to me, the morning Jesus left. "Now I believe, not just because of your testimony – but I have been able to hear it for myself and indeed this is the Saviour of the world."

"I agree," said another and many others' voices followed suit. For the first time in many years, I felt happy.

....

I continued to hear about Jesus. I heard a while later that on his way to Jerusalem one day, Jesus had sent messengers ahead to make arrangements for accommodation but the villagers refused and he moved on somewhere else. But I know Jesus still continued to try and bridge the divide between the Samaritans and Jews. Someone told me of his story about a Samaritan traveller being the one to show care for an injured Jewish man, and also another story when a Samaritan leper was the only one, out of ten lepers healed, to return to thank him. Jesus didn't hide the fact that the man was a Samaritan but he spoke out about it.

That's why I couldn't believe he was dead, that day when Galiano told me. Little did I know, that was not the end of the story but only the start.

....

Apparently, after his death his followers went to the tomb on the third day and he wasn't there! Just completely disappeared! This was followed by sightings of Jesus in many different places. Then people saw him being taken up to heaven, but before he went he promised them that he would leave the Holy Spirit with them. The Holy Spirit? I remember he spoke about the Holy Spirit that day we all went to the well.

And this Holy Spirit did come as he promised. It was at the Feast of Pentecost. There was a sound of a gale force wind filling the room and everyone started speaking in other languages than their own. I can't imagine what it was like there. People from all over the world were there and came running to the room. When they heard their own language being spoken, everyone was awestruck.

Much happened after that. We heard all these things second hand, but it ignited our faith in a new way as we heard by word of mouth about the teaching of his followers, the birth of many new churches and hundreds of miracles around the area.

There were some who hated the new believers and then persecution began. A follower of Jesus called Philip had come down to Samaria away from the persecution. We were so excited as we travelled across the country to see him. There were crowds of people there, many of whom had never seen Jesus and yet still believed in him. When we arrived, there were miracles happening everywhere and so much noise and excitement. Unclean spirits were screaming out as they left those who were possessed. There was a paralysed man I saw just get up and walk, in fact I actually witnessed several lame men and women get up and begin to run around. People just followed Philip wherever he went. People were laughing and shouting and talking, both men and women together. It's a day I will just never forget.

Even Simon, who was a notorious magician, came to see Philip speaking out the good news and baptising people. Everyone had forgotten about him in the excitement of these real life miracles. And then Simon believed and was baptised. It was all so unreal. He followed Philip everywhere watching the miracles he did with such awe and wonder. We were over in that area a few days and the apostles Peter and John came down to visit us. When they arrived, they moved amongst the crowd laying hands on us all one after the other. When Peter put his hands on my head, it was like a wave of power rushed through me from my head to my feet and I began to speak in another language I didn't understand.

Later, I saw the apostles praying for Simon the magician. Apparently he was now deep in repentance after offering to buy the effects of laying on of hands from the apostles! If only he understood.

....

The Story of the Woman at the Well

All that was a long time ago. My time has been spent since then, sharing the news of Jesus with everyone I meet. I cannot stay quiet.

I don't know how long I have left on this earth but I'm not scared of the future anymore. I know that fairly soon I will meet Jesus again but this time, by the eternal well. The well where we first met will not be there forever, but his eternal well *will* last forever and when I arrive, he will look at me and I at him and he will say those words again...

"Woman, the water I gave you, indeed became a well of water continually springing up within you, giving you eternal life.

Now. This is that eternal life. Welcome..."

I can't wait!

The Well and The Woman

The Woman at the Well

Taken from *The Message* Bible

Jesus realized that the Pharisees were keeping count of the baptisms that he and John performed (although his disciples, not Jesus, did the actual baptizing). They had posted the score that Jesus was ahead, turning him and John into rivals in the eyes of the people. So Jesus left the Judean countryside and went back to Galilee.

To get there, he had to pass through Samaria. He came into Sychar, a Samaritan village that bordered the field Jacob had given his son Joseph. Jacob's well was still there. Jesus, worn out by the trip, sat down at the well. It was noon.

A woman, a Samaritan, came to draw water. Jesus said, "Would you give me a drink of water?" (His disciples had gone to the village to buy food for lunch.)

The Samaritan woman, taken aback, asked, "How come you, a Jew, are asking me, a Samaritan woman, for a drink?" (Jews in those days wouldn't be caught dead talking to Samaritans.)

Jesus answered, "If you knew the generosity of God and who I am, you would be asking me for a drink, and I would give you fresh, living water."

The Well and The Woman

The woman said, "Sir, you don't even have a bucket to draw with, and this well is deep. So how are you going to get this 'living water'? Are you a better man than our ancestor Jacob, who dug this well and drank from it, he and his sons and livestock, and passed it down to us?"

Jesus said, "Everyone who drinks this water will get thirsty again and again. Anyone who drinks the water I give will never thirst – not ever. The water I give will be an artesian spring within, gushing fountains of endless life."

The woman said, "Sir, give me this water so I won't ever get thirsty, won't ever have to come back to this well again!"

He said, "Go call your husband and then come back."

"I have no husband," she said.

"That's nicely put: 'I have no husband.' You've had five husbands, and the man you're living with now isn't even your husband. You spoke the truth there, sure enough."

"Oh, so you're a prophet! Well, tell me this: Our ancestors worshiped God at this mountain, but you Jews insist that Jerusalem is the only place for worship, right?"

"Believe me, woman, the time is coming when you Samaritans will worship the Father neither here at this mountain nor there in Jerusalem. You worship guessing in the dark; we Jews worship in the clear light of day. God's way of salvation is made available through the Jews. But the time is coming – it has, in fact, come – when what you're called will not matter and where you go to worship will not matter.

"It's who you are and the way you live that count before God. Your worship must engage your spirit in the pursuit of truth. That's the kind of people the Father is out looking for: those who are simply and honestly themselves before him in

their worship. God is sheer being itself – Spirit. Those who worship him must do it out of their very being, their spirits, their true selves, in adoration."

The woman said, "I don't know about that. I do know that the Messiah is coming. When he arrives, we'll get the whole story."

"I am he," said Jesus. "You don't have to wait any longer or look any further."

Just then his disciples came back. They were shocked. They couldn't believe he was talking with that kind of a woman. No one said what they were all thinking, but their faces showed it.

The woman took the hint and left. In her confusion she left her water pot. Back in the village she told the people, "Come see a man who knew all about the things I did, who knows me inside and out. Do you think this could be the Messiah?" And they went out to see for themselves.

Many of the Samaritans from that village committed themselves to him because of the woman's witness: "He knew all about the things I did. He knows me inside and out!" They asked him to stay on, so Jesus stayed two days. A lot more people entrusted their lives to him when they heard what he had to say. They said to the woman, "We're no longer taking this on your say-so. We've heard it for ourselves and know it for sure. He's the Saviour of the world!"

After the two days he left for Galilee.

John 4:1-45

The Well and The Woman

1

The Well of Life

Jesus, worn out by the trip, sat down at the well.

John 4:6

A little while ago, I received a present from a friend and as with all presents, I wanted to find out what was in it. When I opened it, I found it was a DVD about *Well Dressings at Tissington, Derbyshire,* near where we used to visit. It was special to me because many years ago, Lynne and I used to go with my parents to see the Tissington Well Dressings. Later I watched the DVD and it brought back so many memories of the times when we walked through the main street and admired the wells, both real and imitation, beautifully decorated with thousands of brightly coloured flower petals. Each petal was lovingly and carefully placed, making up a picture of every kind of scene you might imagine. We sometimes peered down the wells which reached right down deep into the ground producing their life giving water long ago.

And the story of this book takes place at a well. But it wasn't a decorated well. It was just an ordinary well where the women went to draw water every day.

The Well and The Woman

If you were to look through the Bible, you would see it is full of events which took place by a well. Wells were hugely significant in Bible times because it was the well that produced water and sustained life. There were no taps, just the village well.

Wells were hugely precious too. If an enemy wanted to overpower a village, they could simply block up the well and the people would die from lack of water.

We see the Philistines do this in Genesis:

> *Isaac planted crops in that land and took in a huge harvest. God blessed him. The man got richer and richer by the day until he was very wealthy. He accumulated flocks and herds and many, many servants, so much so that the Philistines began to envy him. They got back at him by throwing dirt and debris into all the wells that his father's servants had dug back in the days of his father Abraham, clogging up all the wells.*

Genesis 26:12-15

We see how quarrels began over wells:

> *One day, as Isaac's servants were digging in the valley, they came on a well of spring water. The shepherds of Gerar quarrelled with Isaac's shepherds, claiming, "This water is ours." So Isaac named the well Esek (Quarrel) because they quarrelled over it. They dug another well and there was a difference over that one also, so he named it Sitnah (Accusation). He went on from there and dug yet another well. But there was no fighting over this one so he named it Rehoboth (Wide-Open Spaces), saying, "Now God has given us plenty of space to spread out in the land."*

Genesis 26:19-22

We see that if people wanted to pass through a certain area, they would promise not to drink from the local well:

> *"Will you give us permission to cut across your land? We won't trespass through your fields or orchards and we won't drink out of your wells; we'll keep to the main road, the King's Road, straying neither right nor left until we've crossed your border."*
>
> *The king of Edom answered, "Not on your life. If you so much as set a foot on my land, I'll kill you."*
>
> *The People of Israel said, "Look, we'll stay on the main road. If we or our animals drink any water, we'll pay you for it. We're harmless – just a company of footsore travellers."*

> Numbers 20:17-19

There were, indeed, few things which were more important to daily life than the village well, not only in Bible lands but many years ago in our own land also.

If you were to study the *National Well Record Archive* you would discover that there are over 105,000 records of springs, water wells and water boreholes in England, Wales and Scotland, and the significance of these things originated a long time before Christianity. When people dug a well, it became a special place due to the fact that, before running water, it really was the source of life itself. There was no other way of staying alive!

When missionaries first arrived in Britain they saw the people visit wells to make offerings, to seek wisdom, solve problems and even talk to their dead relatives there. The missionaries watched this behaviour for a while and then in time they Christianised it, encouraging the people to thank God for the water these wells provided. And so the wells became a part of Christianity.

There were always two types of well, some created by men with much blood, sweat and toil, and some created by nature when water worked its way up to gaps in the rocks and eventually penetrated the surface.

In our own Christian experience, sometimes we have to persevere and work hard to reach God but at other times, He unexpectedly bursts into our life and our experience. I'm sure that you could tell of both experiences.

But wells don't just appear and thrive. They need attention.

Wells need discovering

There was an article in the newspaper a little while ago which read as follows:

> *A few days into a well-deserved holiday a couple received a phone call from a builder friend who was helping them restore their home in a country village. It was the year 2000 and with a four year long restoration of the old house complete, they had turned their attention to the garden.*
>
> *The builder told them that during the clearing of the area for a patio at the back of the house an ancient well had been found and he asked if the couple wanted it filled in. "No," said the couple straight away, and there were many other discoveries, such as murals hidden beneath layers of wallpaper and an ancient pub sign from long ago. But the well became their most precious find.*

And in a similar way, when we are forced, or choose to dig deep in God, we find treasures we didn't expect. Sometimes, it can cost effort and heartache but there are things to find in Him. God's attributes are unfathomable and we can never reach the end of his amazing surprises if we are willing to search for them. That's what keeps our journey fresh and living because there is always something new to discover, however long ago we began our spiritual journey.

Do you need to start to search for those treasures, to desire to see things you've never seen and hear things you've never heard?

Take a moment to meditate on the verse below and see what God personally says to you:

> *Joyfully you'll pull up buckets of water from the wells of salvation and as you do it, you'll say, "Give thanks to God."*

Isaiah 12:3-4

That means we can keep enjoying the living water again and again. We can keep pulling up buckets of the Holy Spirit and treasures in Him by which we can be refreshed every day.

Wells need hard work

We have a friend who, for thirty years, used to work in the village of Woodingdean, a place which had the deepest 'hand dug' well in the world. Its depth was greater than the height of the Empire State Building. When they were digging the well, the builders built platforms every few hundred metres down. It seemed that they would be digging forever but they knew that eventually they would reach water.

It took four years but at the end of that period of back breaking work, it was March 1862 when one morning, they noticed the earth starting to be pushed up. As fast as they could they began to scramble back up the rickety ladders and platforms to get to the top before the water broke through and filled the 1,285 feet they had so patiently dug.

There must have been times they thought they would never reach the water and for you, maybe you've been digging and searching but there is no sign of that fresh living water you once experienced. Sometimes, the source of life is reached by descending into the depths of a deep dark shaft and maybe you're there. If so, then you are in the very place where the living water can be found. Maybe that water is nearer than you think.

Why not take time now to meditate on the verse below and see what God says personally to you as you do?

> *Hey there! All who are thirsty, come to the water! Are you penniless? Come anyway – buy and eat. Come buy your drinks, buy wine and milk, buy without money, everything's free.*

> Isaiah 55:1

Here, you are invited to *come* and to *come* is an action. To come means to *move nearer, to approach, to arrive, to reach*. It's something we *do* and as we do that, we get nearer to the source of life.

Wells need maintenance

Apparently, when a well had been dug, the first five to ten years were taken to scrub the walls of the well to make sure it was clean for water to stand in and then even after that, every five years, it was scrubbed again. Children, no doubt, had a choice in those days, down the well or up the chimney!

How do we maintain our relationship or our *well* with God? We maintain it by regularly spending time with him, reading his word, becoming part of a healthy church and spending time in fellowship with other Christians. It's how we keep things alive, it's how we keep our well from getting covered with moss, poison ivy and falling into disrepair. These are the things that keep us moving in the right direction.

It's important that we maintain our well. It's the thing that brings us life on a daily basis and it's vital it's maintained. It's so easy for it to get neglected or overgrown.

Retreats and time away are also good things to do. In Exodus (15:27), the children of Israel came to Elim where there were twelve springs of water and seventy palm trees. They set up camp by the water. Maybe we all need an Elim! To regularly set up camp somewhere to be refreshed and renewed in God in different surroundings.

Keep maintaining your well. Keep putting in the hard work, protecting that which God began in you on the day you were saved. Widen your well, increase the depth of your well, strengthen the walls of your well and most of all utilise your well. For He is the source of life and the source of all you live for.

Maybe take time to meditate on the verse below and see what God says personally to you:

> *Nobody hungry, nobody thirsty, shade from the sun, shelter from the wind. For the compassionate one guides them, takes them to the best springs.*

> Isaiah 49:10

That is His promise to you and I, the best springs in God.

Wells need protection

While writing about wells, I've been doing a little research on what I would do if I owned a well. Living on an estate in East Kilbride, Scotland, I don't think I'm likely to be digging a well but if I did, I wouldn't just be digging a hole in the ground and leaving it. There are several things the law would require me to do.

Firstly, I would need to test the water regularly to check it was pure. I would need to identify problems from the immediate ground such as fertilisers, livestock or motor oil. I would need to identify potential problems from the community like new building sites, pesticides on fields and salt sprayed on the roads. I would need to do these things to protect my well from harm.

I wonder, how many things can pollute the well of our *God experience?* Things we see, hear, think or read? We are called to be in the world but not of the world. When we were first saved, it was easy in a sense. We were told *"don't drink, dance, spit or chew or hang around with those that do!"* Nowadays the pendulum has swung and we are encouraged to get out there and be with the people. But the question I must always ask is: Am I any different from them? Do I dissolve into them when I'm with them and do I allow the things I see and hear to pollute the living water in me? What about you?

Maybe take time to meditate on the verse below and see what God says personally to you:

> *Guard this precious thing placed in your custody by the Holy Spirit who works in us.*

> 2 Timothy 1:14

In a way, when you think about the whole concept of digging deep into God for the water of life, it's really just a rehearsal.

Revelation 22:1 reads:

> *Then the Angel showed me the Water of Life River; crystal bright. It flowed from the throne of God and the Lamb right down the middle of the street.*

The Well of Life

The source, the place to which we are digging, is the Water of Life River which we find deep in God. That is the place where earth touches heaven and where heaven touches earth.

The well dressings in Tissington began after the Black Death of 1348 when five million people died. That was sixty per cent of the entire population of Europe. But in Tissington, everyone escaped. Not one person died and their immunity was ascribed to the purity of the water supply. As a result, ever since for nearly seven hundred years, they have dressed their wells as a symbol of thanksgiving to God.

Today we don't have a visible Black Death. But in a sense we do have an invisible one; things that are eating away at the values we have held for centuries. The thing that will keep us strong in these times, is the purity of the water of life river. As we dig wells all over the country, it gives opportunity for other people to get drenched by that water. If it can happen to others, it can happen here. Will you start digging again?

Will you *discover* your well, *work hard* on it, *maintain* it and *protect* it?

Because that water of life river inside you is the most precious thing you have.

....

Consider:

1. Is there more to discover?

2. Do you need to work on your well?

3. Does your well need a regular programme of maintenance?

4. How can you protect your well?

2

Out in the Noonday Sun

And it was noon....

John 4:6

I was sorting through the spare room one day, where I keep my stock of books. And as I sorted out the boxes, I realised the books I write are all about stories. I'd never really thought about it before but *Across the Brook* tells the individual stories of Kevin and I and of God's invisible hand in our early lives during the 1950s and 60s. *Dear Sally* is the story of our first couple of years in the city of Glasgow when I wrote letters to a friend, as God was teaching me painful principles by which I would learn to live. *The White Elephant* and *The Seagull* are two books full of stories of Glaswegians who we loved and were our inspiration as we pastored our church. *Great Thoughts From a Little Dog* is a daily devotional for dog lovers. *A Family at War*, the story of my own family, generations ago during the war years, likens their battles to our own spiritual warfare as Christians. Lastly, *The Journey* contains some personal life stories illustrating truths God is constantly teaching us on our journey through life.

Whoever you are, you have a story. Your story is a collection of 'happenings' which are personal to you alone and there is one very big reason that your story is special. It's not because of what it contains but because of the simple fact that *no one can take it away from you*. Most other things in our life can be stolen from us; our health, our wealth, our possessions, our spouse and even our life. But nothing and no one can take away your story. They can change it, yes, but you will always have a story. God has ordained the day it will begin and the day it will end on this earth and between those days it belongs to you!

And you are writing that story. Life events take place, but by our actions and our reactions, by our choices both good and bad, you and I determine a lot of what happens in our story.

Stories Are Everywhere

Stories are all around us. We get home in the evening and if we have other people in the house or if we phone or text them, we tell stories of the people we met that day. When we meet a friend for coffee, we tell stories that have happened to us since we last met.

Children love stories and from as soon as they can understand, their life is filled with stories and sometimes, the same story over and over and over again!

Stories help people connect with each other. If you stand next to someone at a bus stop and they begin to talk to you and tell you about their mother in hospital, they become a person. You feel more connected to them, than to the person who, wearing headphones, stares at the pavement. Stories make connections.

Scientists have even proved that when someone tells a story, the listener's brain responses, mirror the storyteller's brain patterns.

Stories are everywhere. Shops and libraries are full of novels, TV is full of reality shows and interviews about real people and real life. The adverts at Christmas tell the story of *a little rabbit who feels sorry for a bear with no presents and discovers that John Lewis is a great place to shop.* Films tell stories and have become a multi-million pound industry. In the courtroom, a testimony is often the thing that wins the case and the police are always looking for witnesses to tell their *story.*

One of my hobbies is family research and a while back, I found out that many years ago my great-grandfather travelled with his family from Italy to the UK and they made a home here. It was better than the poverty of Italy at that time, but they were still very poor until they began to earn a living and progress up the ladder of life. He had seven children and when they grew up, they went to live in Australia, all except my grandfather. So my mum and her siblings grew up here and my grandfather's siblings had their children and grandchildren in Australia.

Last year we received an email from one of those grandchildren. And as we were going to Australia that summer, we met up with cousins in Sydney, Brisbane, Adelaide and Darwin. What was amazing was that they all had a story! Just as I had been living my story across the world, there were people who looked a bit like me and thought a bit like me who had a story as well. And we told our stories and those stories crossed barriers of time, of distance, of culture and of age, as we shared them together.

Stories do amazing things. As Jesus told stories, the brain responses of the people around Him were connecting to the brain patterns of Jesus! They connected people with Him to help them understand what He was saying. He knew the power of a story, long before it had ever been proved.

And you have a story. Whoever you are, wherever you have come from, whatever you've been doing, however old you may be, your story is important because it is unique.

The woman who came to the well had a story. This woman has no name but she was a real person with a real name, a real identity and a real story just like you and I, and some important things happened to her. One of which was that she had the longest recorded conversation with Jesus of anyone in the Bible. She met Jesus and she actually entered into a debate with Him. She didn't wait for permission to speak, she just spoke with Him as an intellectual equal.

You will know that this woman was from a despised group of people and even within that group she was ostracised, because she had been married five times and the man she was currently living with wasn't her husband. That's a story!

Jesus was living His story and the woman was making hers. And one day, they met.

It was midday and we know that He had sent the disciples to the village to buy food for lunch while He waited by the well. And as He stood there He saw her arriving.

Now this activity at the well was usually the social highlight of a woman's day when they caught up with all the news, took advice about their kids and swapped recipes and all that. But the woman was alone because she had maybe chosen to go there at noon when it was so hot that no one else was around.

And the words that Jesus spoke to her would begin the rest of her life. It would change her story. This man she had never met was about to transform her story when He asked *"Woman, would you give me a drink of water?"* She had no idea but two thousand years later, we are here reading about her. How amazing is that?

He was waiting

Jesus sat down waiting for the woman to arrive but she had not been aware of that. She would probably have been getting her water pot prepared, sweeping the floor and preparing food. But she had a date with destiny.

Jesus has been waiting for you to arrive, for *you* to reach this moment. When you woke this morning, when you picked up this book, when you started to read, He was waiting for you. He already has it all planned out because He has words to speak to you, things to reveal to you and challenges to make to you.

Jesus has been waiting for this moment in order to intervene in your story. That's what He's doing. He could be going to enhance your story, or maybe to change the direction of your story or strengthen you in your story, but whoever you are, wherever you are from, nothing is by chance when you are open to Him. He has planned it all.

It was noon

Secondly, the Bible says it was noon. The sun was very hot and maybe in your situation and circumstances, you stand in the noonday sun. You are thirsty, you are worn out, you feel like you have walked for miles. Maybe you feel you have emotional sunburn, mental blisters or heat exhaustion or you have just been too busy? Noon is a hectic time of the day. Most people don't have their feet up at noon!

I want to ask you, do you need to stand in His shade today? Remember that *"he who dwells in the shelter of the Most High will rest in the shadow of the Almighty"* (Psalm 91:1). Remember that He will keep you in perfect peace when your mind is fixed on Him.

Do you need to stand in that shelter today? Do you need to rest in the shadow of the Almighty right now? Do you need to fix your mind on Him and soak in His peace at this moment? Why not do that right now?

She was coming

And then the Bible says a *"woman from Samaria came"*. Is that you? Whether male or female, have you come? Could we say a man called Steven, Brian, Callum? A woman called Linda, Maureen? Kirsty? Whoever you are, you have come to this moment.

But we can *arrive* somewhere but not *be* somewhere.

When we were first saved Kevin and I went to a Brethren church and it taught us many good things, but we were young and sometimes the services were hard to sit through. It was difficult to understand what some of the speakers were talking about and sometimes it got pretty boring.

So we invented little games to brighten up the meeting.

When Chippy Watts got up each week, he would pray the longest prayers we had ever heard! Each week they seemed to get longer and longer. So we would take bets on the length of the prayer. We would write our bet on a piece of paper and someone would time the prayer.

One speaker was called Mr Blakehurst and we called him "The Dear Friend" because he would end nearly every sentence with the words "Dear Friends". We would count the number of times he said it to see if he broke his record from his last visit. We had all sorts of ways of keeping ourselves amused.

There was one unfortunate Sunday evening which was the final of the FA cup. That didn't bother me at all but Kevin wasn't at all keen on missing it so he arrived with his transistor radio, and an ear piece in his pocket. Once the sermon had begun he settled down comfortably with his ear piece in to enjoy the football.

And all went well until...Bobby Moore passed the ball to Alan Ball. Ball beat two players in an amazing dribble and passed the ball to Bobby Charlton who squared it to Alan Mullery. Mullery, quick as a flash, pulled back his right foot and SHOT!!! The ball flew like a rocket past the German goalkeeper and burst into the back of the net.

At that moment, sixty thousand people AND Kevin jumped to their feet in ecstasy! Kevin came down to earth right in the middle of Mr Blakehurst's third point! It was not a happy experience for any of us!!

You see we were *there* but we *weren't* there. And we can be *here* but we're *not* here. You can be reading but your mind is elsewhere.

I wonder how Jesus felt when He saw she'd come and was listening to Him? You see, He knew her life was going to change and the rest would be history.

I wonder how God feels right now as He sees you've come to this moment and are open for Him to speak to you? You see He knows He has adjustments to make to your story.

You *listen* to My story.

You *listen* to Her story.

But you *live* your story...and He has been waiting for you to arrive.

And just as He adjusted *her* story, He wants to adjust *your* story today; to give you more direction, to tell you He's with you, to give you some shade from the sun so you can move onward and upward.

....

Consider:

1. Why not think for five minutes about the fact that everything is planned by Him and that He has been waiting for you to come to Him?

2. Consider:

> Do you stand in the noonday sun? Are you thirsty, worn out? Do you feel like you have walked for miles?

> Do you feel you have emotional sunburn? How? Mental blisters? Why? Heat exhaustion? What's the cause?

> Have you just been too busy? What with?

3. Why not become fully present in this moment and tell Him you are waiting and ready for whatever He wants to do afresh in your life?

3

God's Secret Weapon

A woman, a Samaritan, came to draw water. Jesus said,
"Would you give me a drink of water?"

John 4:7

Wherever in the world you live you will find people who are connected through Facebook, WhatsApp, Snapchat and Twitter. It no longer matters whether you live across the road, or across the world, you can be friends and be in daily contact.

But the truth is, that despite all this social media, people have probably never been more isolated. In this day and age, relatives often live miles away, neighbourhoods are not the supportive places they once were and friends are often so busy. We have never been more connected yet for some, they have never been more isolated.

But I believe that as Christians, we could have a secret weapon in our hands which can break through that isolation.

In our story, we see Jesus, a Jew, and the woman, a Samaritan. The Samaritans were hated by the Jews, they were considered a heretical Jewish cult who had mingled pagan idolatrous practices with the Law of Moses. They were hated even more than the Gentiles. In fact, the Jews had a prayer in which they said, "Thank God I am not a Samaritan". So in a cultural sense Jesus shouldn't have been speaking to a Samaritan, certainly not to a woman and definitely not to a Samaritan woman, living with a man who wasn't her husband.

When Jesus saw this woman, however, He was filled with something that meant the barriers of gender, race, religion and lifestyle didn't matter, and that something was EMPATHY.

Could *empathy* be a secret fire lighter of God?

I don't know if you've ever used fire lighters. Some years ago Kevin and I went to take a few days away in a country cottage. It seemed a great idea at the time but what I hadn't bargained for, was a *real* fire. But with the conviction that anything is possible if you believe, we took the paper, coal and wood and lit it. The tiny little match burned for a few seconds, then went out. So we did it again. And again. And again! And we were freezing.

Eventually I phoned my mum and asked, "Do you know how to make a fire?" She laughed as she had been doing it for fifty years. "Go and get some firelighters," she advised. So we did and before long we had a lovely blazing fire in the hearth. Making a fire seemed so difficult but with the right tools, suddenly we were expert fire lighters.

And as you read this chapter I want to ask you, could *empathy* be a secret fire lighter of God? As we take time to ask about a colleague's sick mother more often than we do, as we make an effort to ask about the health problems of the elderly gent next door, as we listen to the problems of the shop keeper down the road, could a bridge be built for God to walk across?

Just before Christmas, Kevin and I were going Christmas shopping and we were walking down into the town. On the way, Kevin called in a shop and while standing outside, I noticed that at the tram stop sat an old man who lifted his hand, smiled and waved as I walked past. I returned the wave and stood outside the shop to wait for Kevin.

After a minute or so of watching the elderly gent, himself watching the cars pass by, I wandered over and began to talk to him. He patted the bench beside him so I sat down. After passing comment about the weather, I told him that I was waiting for my husband and we were going to go Christmas shopping. He said that's nice and then added, "I'm waiting for my wife. Once she comes, we're going Christmas shopping too. She's coming at half past eleven." It was eleven then but he was very well wrapped up I noticed and had a cushion to sit on. Within a minute Kevin emerged from the shop and we said goodbye and went on our way.

I forgot the old man until we were on our way home in the car a couple of hours later when I saw him still sitting at the same tram stop with his walking frame and cushion.

It was later that day when I started to think about it that the realisation hit me! I started to tell Kevin about our conversation earlier that day but as I shared, I realised – there was no wife and there was no Christmas shopping and maybe even no Christmas. Then something happened to me, a large lump came in my throat, my voice wavered and tears filled my eyes...empathy had hit me. I thought about the old man. I realised his situation. It affected me emotionally.

Empathy is the ability to recognise others' experiences and have the emotional ability to respond. It is the mental action of taking yourself out of your own shoes and putting yourself in the shoes of others, stepping outside your tiny world and stepping into theirs.

Empathy is not sympathy. Sympathy sort of distances you from someone in a way saying *"I am better than you"*.

Empathy draws you towards someone saying *"I am down here with you".*

So could empathy be a weapon which could penetrate the enemy's defences and those barriers that people put around themselves?

Our Human Empathy

As individuals, we are all wired up differently and we respond differently to people. Some people are very easily moved by the plight of others, they can sit and watch the news and they are there in that place with them. Some are not.

Empathy can often be determined by your passion and your experience too. I feel compassion when I read articles in the paper about elderly people in traumatic situations, about younger people lonely and alone, about cruelty to animals. But tell me stories about other things and I show empathy by choice, not by feeling. For you it might be refugees, or children in poverty or prisoners. Everyone is different and there are things you are moved by and other situations that maybe, you have to make a choice to show empathy.

Human beings can be anywhere on the empathy spectrum ranging from one extreme, totally self-absorbed, to the other, an inability to see anything but the point of view of the other person.

I am a primary school teacher and deal with a whole variety of parents. Some say about their children:

"I know what my son is like. Don't tell me what he's like. I live with him. How you put up with him all day, I have no idea!"

Others parents say:

"If Samuel says he didn't do it, then he didn't do it!" And even though I've watched Samuel do it and thirty other children have seen Samuel do it, there's nothing that I can say, which will convince Mrs Smith that her son did it!

I had a mother-in-law who was perfect in nearly every way. Apart from one! And this was it: she could not see any fault whatsoever in her son!

For example one Christmas we were seated around the table having Christmas dinner. There was Kevin, his brother and wife, his niece and his mum and myself. At the end of the meal, I helped to clear up, and around where Kevin had been seated, under his chair the floor was littered with bits of turkey. Everyone else's bit of floor was clean but Kevin's was covered in bits of his dinner.

"Look at your mum's floor," I said light-heartedly, as I picked up the bits. "You've made a right mess!"

"Oh no, our Marg," said his mum immediately defensive.

"It's not our Kev's fault. I cooked that turkey myself this morning and it's a *particularly crumbly turkey!*"

At the other extreme are people whose world revolves totally around themselves. We are all the centre of our world to some extent but hopefully as we grow up and mature, we understand that there are other people in this world too, and we learn to extend our view point and conversation beyond ourselves.

The blessing of a friendship is the sharing of yourself, but also the sharing of the other person. So if you want to make more friends, then maybe ask more questions!

When I meet my best friend, we talk. She asks about Kevin then I ask about Phil. She asks about my job and I ask about the grandkids. She asks about my holiday and I ask about hers.

It's how it works! Lynne came up for three days recently when Kevin was away.

"What did you do?" Kevin asked me when he arrived home.

"Well... we talked."

"What else?"

"Well... we talked..."

"Anything else?"

"Well nothing really, we just talked..." He looked at me in amazement.

"How can you *possibly* talk for three whole days? And do nothing else?"

"Well it just happens," I replied. "You know, I say something, then Lynne says something, then I say something, then Lynne says something and the time just sort of...goes...you know?" He just regarded me with a strange look on his face.

This ability to give our attention to other people is a huge deal in the Bible, to imagine another person's thoughts and feelings and to have the drive to respond with an appropriate emotion and action.

Look at the following verses:

> *If one part hurts, every other part is involved in the hurt, and in the healing. If one part flourishes, every other part enters into the exuberance.*

> 1 Corinthians 12:26

That's EMPATHY

> *Share their burdens, and so complete Christ's law.*

> Galatians 6:2

That's EMPATHY

Laugh with your happy friends when they're happy; share tears when they're down.

Romans 12:15

That's EMPATHY

Regard prisoners as if you were in prison with them. Look on victims of abuse as if what happened to them had happened to you.

Hebrews 3:13

That's EMPATHY

Love others as well as you love yourself.

Mark 12:31

That's EMPATHY

Showing empathy, is something that God clearly wants us to do, in order to connect and share His love with those around us.

That's Human Empathy.

God's Divine Empathy

But we can't give if we haven't received.

Think physically first of all. Someone gives you money and you give money to someone else. Physically, unless you have received possessions, food, clothes, you cannot give them away. You cannot materialise things out of nothing. You need to have received, in order to give.

And we know it's the same emotionally. Every time you look at the life of a disturbed child or an adult, there is a reason. They are lacking in something. I'm sure you've read about instances of people who have committed horrendous crimes and felt no regret, because they are unable to put themselves into someone else's shoes. In fact, part of prison rehabilitation now, is helping the offender put themselves in the position of the victim and *empathise.*

The world is waking up more to the importance of empathy. Apparently empathy has been identified as one of the most important leadership skills of the twenty-first century.

Browns University in the USA teaches a whole two week course on *Empathy.* Also you are now able to take a test called the Baron Cohen Test which will give you your empathy quotient. How amazing that we open the New Testament, written two thousand years ago, and it's all already written down there.

There is a space inside each of us which needs to be filled with our basic needs of security, safety, belonging, achievement and the knowledge that we are loved... and if this space is not filled, we are forever trying to satisfy that need and our life gets messed up.

The great news is that when we belong to God and to His family, what we have lacked from human sources, our Heavenly Father is more than able to make up any lack we have.

When Jesus was on earth, He became a visible illustration of God's compassion and empathy to everyone.

Look at the following verses:

Luke writes,

> *Just then a woman of the village, the town harlot, having learned that Jesus was a guest in the home of the Pharisee, came with a bottle of very expensive perfume and stood at his feet, weeping, raining tears on his feet. Letting down her hair, she*

dried his feet, kissed them, and anointed them with the perfume.

Then he spoke to her: "I forgive your sins."

Luke 7:37-38,48

That's EMPATHY.

John writes,

The religion scholars and Pharisees led in a woman who had been caught in an act of adultery.

They kept at him, badgering him. He straightened up and said, "The sinless one among you, go first: Throw the stone."

John 8:3,7

That's EMPATHY.

Luke also writes,

In the crowd that day there was a woman who for twelve years had been afflicted with haemorrhages. She had spent every penny she had on doctors but not one had been able to help her. She slipped in from behind and touched the edge of Jesus' robe. At that very moment her haemorrhaging stopped. Jesus said, "Who touched me?"...

Jesus said, "Daughter, you took a risk trusting me, and now you're healed and whole. Live well, live blessed!"

Luke 8:43-44,48

That's EMPATHY.

Matthew writes,

Then Jesus made a circuit of all the towns and villages. He taught in their meeting places, reported kingdom news, and healed their diseased bodies, healed their bruised and hurt lives. When he looked out over the crowds, his heart broke. So confused and aimless they were, like sheep with no shepherd.

Matthew 9:35-36

That's EMPATHY.

Empathy connects people together.

Empathy gives people a sense of identity connected to yours and they feel greater, they feel less alone.

Empathy heals, it says I care for you.

Empathy builds trust and that's what Jesus was doing.

And just as Jesus had empathy back then, our God has empathy and love right now and God's empathy is not just for the crowds but it's for you. That knowledge isn't a just once and for all revelation but it's something that needs to wash over our heart again and again, somewhat like getting in the shower when we clean off the dust and grime of everyday life.

Did you used to know God's empathy and love washing through your heart? Do you need to visit that again?

When we regularly immerse ourselves in the knowledge that God feels empathy and love and compassion towards us, then it has the effect of washing from us those experiences that cause us to become hard and uncaring and unforgiving. It keeps our heart soft.

Do you *really* know and experience God's empathy for you every day? Not for yesterday or tomorrow but for you, today? That you are special to Him, that you matter to Him and that He is right there with you in this life?

God's Secret Weapon

The Word of God is powerful and living and active. Allow these powerful and living words to wash over you right now:

> *If your heart is broken, you'll find God right there; if you're kicked in the gut, he'll help you catch your breath.*

> Psalm 34:18

> *As a mother comforts her child, so I'll comfort you.*

> Isaiah 66:13

> *Live carefree before God; he is most careful with you.*

> 1 Peter 5:7

> *We do not have a high priest who is unable to sympathise with our weaknesses but one who in every respect has been tempted as we are, yet without sin. Let us draw near that we may receive.*

> Hebrews 4 15-16

So it's God's design that we receive and then we give, otherwise we give and give and if we don't know that special something that comes from above, one day we have nothing left to give.

It's God's design. It's a two part process. He loves. We love.

Here is an illustration, John 15:12:

> *"This is my command: Love one another..."* (show empathy).

Now see what happens before that...

> *"...the way I loved you."*

Christ loved us first, before He ever commanded us to do the loving. We love because He has loved us.

Here is another illustration:

> *"Forgive one another..."* (Ephesians 4:32)

Now see what happens before that...

> *"...as quickly and thoroughly as God in Christ forgave you."*

Christ forgave us first before he ever instructed us to do the forgiving. We can forgive because we have been forgiven.

As our needs are met, so we can meet the needs of others.

The Fire of Fused Empathy

Above, we have explored "our natural empathy" and "God's divine empathy". Could it be when these two things come together that he can actually begin to set hearts on fire through us?

I don't know if, when you were small, you ever took a magnifying glass and paper outside on a sunny day. Can you remember, you reflected the sun onto the newspaper through the glass, you saw a bright dot and made that dot as small as possible? And by concentrating the energy entering the lens to a single point it became sufficient to raise the temperature enough for a chemical reaction to take place and for the newspaper to set alight? Then you could attempt to set other newspapers, or spiders...or the dog next door on fire!!!

In order to complete that experiment, you needed three things: the sun, a magnifying glass and paper. The sun alone wouldn't complete the experiment. The magnifying glass alone wouldn't work. It needed both, for the paper to catch fire.

And I wonder if it's God's design, for God's empathy to shine into us and activate our empathy that as we touch life after life, those hearts will be set on fire.

If we live, only experiencing God's love and empathy then it only affects us and flows nowhere and we get stagnant. If we live, showing empathy for the needs of the world and receiving nothing ourselves, then our works are empty and we get dry.

Could it be, that just as the sun and the glass ignite the paper, that God touching our heart every day with His compassion will then activate our compassion to a new level, in a supernatural way, for those around us in the world and in our church to feel? A way that can keep giving and giving without running dry? A way that can keep soaking and soaking in God's love without becoming stagnant?

What does the Bible say? We read in John 13:34-35;

> *"Let me give you a new command: Love one another..."* (that's our empathy).

> *"In the same way I loved you, you love one another..."* (that's His empathy).

> *"This is how everyone will recognise that you are my disciples—when they see the love you have for each other..."* (that's the result).

> or

> *"Let me give you a new command: Love one another..."* (that's the magnifying glass we hold).

> *"In the same way I loved you, you love one another..."* (that's the sun shining through the glass).

> *"This is how everyone will recognise that you are my disciples – when they see the love you have for each other..."* (that's the paper which sets fire).

The Well and The Woman

At the side of that well long ago, God's love was coming through Jesus into the life of a Samaritan woman and it set her heart on fire and went on to affect many others.

That's what we want isn't it? That in our neighbourhood and church and workplace, the paths are made straight and the glory of the Lord is revealed?

We want the fire of God to burn in those places and in those hearts. Could it be that empathy is God's secret weapon against the enemy and the barriers of isolation that he puts up around people? It's written right through the New Testament. It's the magnifying glass that God can shine through onto life after life, to ignite those people with His fire.

....

Consider:

1. Consider the *paper* around you (that's the people He has put around you every day). Who are they? Why not talk to Him about them now? He may show you others you have never noticed.

2. Consider the *magnifying glass* (your empathy). Do you need to ask Him to increase that empathy? Do you need to take more steps to show compassion and empathy to those people around you as needs arise? Or is the glass in your life foggy or dirty? Do you need to ask Him to clean that? If so, take time to ask Him.

3. Consider the *sun* (the light and life of God). Are you allowing Him to shine into your life? Do you experience that love on a regular basis washing off the dust and grime of each day? Talk to Him about this.

The Well and The Woman

4

A Badge of Promise

The Samaritan woman, taken aback, asked,
"How come you, a Jew, are asking me, a Samaritan woman,
for a drink?"

John 4:9

I was wandering round a supermarket one day and a song came on the speakers, and then the next day I heard it again. Wherever I went I seemed to be hearing the same song. I don't know if you've heard it but every couple of lines, you hear the recurring phrase "I wasn't expecting that..." That's the phrase that kept going round my head and it started me thinking about those things in my life that happened which I wasn't expecting at all. Both good and bad.

The Bible says that the Samaritan woman was *"taken aback"* when Jesus asked her for a drink of water. She wasn't expecting that. Neither was she expecting the total life change that she received that day.

In life, there are always things you don't expect and the longer you live, the more you get. As you look back, you can see the bad things that take place and you say, "I wasn't expecting that...!" An illness, the death of someone close, a divorce, a redundancy, a relationship breakdown...

But there are also things which happen which are good and you exclaim in delight, "I wasn't expecting that...!"

Accepting the 'ANDs'

When I was eight years old, I moved my chair at Sunday School one day for a new little girl to sit beside me and the next day, there she was again, also sitting beside me at school. She is my best friend and we have just celebrated fifty years of best friendship. On that day I moved my chair...I wasn't expecting that!

On the day we left our church at Glasgow to oversee Elim churches throughout Scotland and North West England I began to write down a few of the precious memories we had. Those thoughts became a book and since then there have been seven more books published. On that night I began to write in my notebook, I can tell you, I wasn't expecting that!

We have always had a dog in the house and when our last dog died, due to many travelling commitments, we agreed, no more dogs! I was secretly hoping for another dog, but sadly dog ownership was not possible. Then one morning a friend rang me and said, "I've got a puppy, I've had it for a week and I'm just not into 'pulling things out of its rear end, walking outside in the pouring rain and finding my passport chewed to bits!' If you have my puppy, I'll look after it whenever you need me to." God provided for me, not just a dog but a dog sitter too who loved to have him stay. Wow. God is good! I wasn't expecting that!

The *"ands"* of life, those things that add to our life are great when they come along.

I sat next to a girl in Sunday school AND ...

I started to write down the great memories we had AND...

I wanted a dog AND...

As I look back, there are a whole host of times when I have responded to blessings in my life and said, "I wasn't expecting that!" Wonderful surprises which God has blessed me with.

Beating the 'BUTs'

But there have also been surprises that God has allowed that I wouldn't have chosen. I'm talking now about the *BUTs* in life.

I had a best friend but...

I had a great relationship but...

My husband had a great job but...

In life we get ANDs that bless our faith.

And we get BUTs that test our faith.

The question is this:

In my life, am I defined by the good things that have happened or

am I defined by the bad things that have taken place?

It is a serious question for us all. It is so easy to set up camp by a trauma, a tragedy or a disaster, as we journey through life and physically we move on, but mentally or emotionally we are still tied to that place of long ago.

God's Interventions

There are hundreds of examples in God's Word where God intervenes in the lives of His children in surprising ways.

The Well and The Woman

I googled the phrase "God's surprises in the Bible" and there were many results. So I clicked on the first entry in the list and it read 5,962 surprises of God. Below are just eight of them. Imagine you are here in these moments:

1. The shepherds on the hillside are watching their sheep expecting a quiet night in the mountains and an angel of the Lord nearly scares them witless. The Bible says they were very fearful... What's in their thoughts? "...I WASN'T EXPECTING THAT!"

Read about it in Luke 2:8-12.

2. Mary and Joseph are searching everywhere, worried out of their mind. They've lost Jesus and then they find Him sitting in the Temple asking questions to the teachers of the law. The Bible says that all who heard Him were astonished! In other words, they were thinking "...I WASN'T EXPECTING THAT!"

Read about it in Luke 2:41-48.

3. The boat is in the middle of the sea tossed about by the waves and the disciples are scared and suddenly in the distance, they see Jesus, walking on top of the sea! And they cry out in fear and say (my paraphrase) "...I WASN'T EXPECTING THAT!"

Read about it in Matthew 14:24-27.

4. Jesus is having dinner in Levi's house with a lot of other tax collectors and sinners, and the scribes and the Pharisees see Him. "How is it that He eats with them?" they ask. In other words, "...I WASN'T EXPECTING THAT!"

Read about it in Matthew 9:10-11.

5. Some men bring a paralysed man on a stretcher to be healed, but they can't get in the house as it is packed out

with people. So they make a hole in the roof and lower him in, right in front of Jesus. And Jesus says, "Get up and pick up your bed and go home." They were all amazed and filled with fear and they thought, "...I WASN'T EXPECTING THAT!"

Read about it in Mark 2:3-12.

6. Jesus has died and there is an earthquake, graves come open and believers are raised from the dead, come out of their graves and go to visit people in the cities. The soldiers guarding the tomb look at all this and say, "Wow, this WAS the Son of God...I WASN'T EXPECTING THAT!"

Read about it in Mark 15:37-39.

7. Two men on a road to a place called Emmaus are discussing the death of Jesus and all that has happened since the crucifixion and suddenly Jesus is walking there right by their side. Suddenly, they recognise Him. "...I WASN'T EXPECTING THAT!"

Read about it in Luke 24:28-32.

8. It is a special day, the day of Pentecost and everyone is together and suddenly there comes a huge wind filling the house and fire comes on people's heads as they are filled with the Holy Spirit and speak in other languages. They are amazed and marvel together "...I WASN'T EXPECTING THAT!"

Read about it in Acts 2:5-12.

The Bible is full of instances where in one way or another people were saying, thinking or feeling those words "...I WASN'T EXPECTING THAT!"

Don't Camp Out

In our story, firstly we see Jesus ask the woman for a drink of water.

Note that Jesus wanted her to do something for Him. He was asking her to act. "Give Me..." He said.

The Bible says that *she was taken aback*. In other words, she was thinking "I wasn't expecting that".

And I wonder, as He said to the lady at the well, "Give me..." what does He ask you and I to "Give me" today? I wonder, could it be those BUTs in our life that we have collected over the years? The BUTs that have made such an impression on us that they have maybe defined our life a little bit? They are the things we always look back to as, *that didn't work for me* or *that didn't happen for me.*

Sometimes we can camp at the BUTs in our life. I was twenty five when my mum died. After that I always thought longingly of those who lost parents much later in life. It took me a long time to register the fact that there are also people, maybe some of you, that lost their mum when they were fifteen or five or even at birth. At that point of realisation, I ceased to camp at that BUT and moved on.

Secondly, Jesus said, "Go call your husband and then come back."

I guess the first thing she thought was, "Oh no, I wasn't expecting that..."

Here we see, not that Jesus wanted her to do something for Him, but that Jesus wanted to do something for her. He wanted to clean up her life but He knew something was holding her back.

What does Jesus want to do for you? Could it be that He wants to clean up your life from the effects of those BUTs but not just that, that He wants to give you more ANDs as you let go of those detestable BUTs.

And then the following takes place. She went back to the village and exclaimed, "Come and meet a man who told me everything I ever did, who knows me inside and out". As a result she saw that many of the Samaritans from that village committed themselves to Him because of her witness. I have a feeling that she would be thinking, "I wasn't expecting that!"

Also, as she did something for Jesus...Jesus did something for her, we see that together, they brought blessing to other people. That's how it works – as we do something for Jesus and give Him those BUTs. As Jesus does something for us and blesses us with those ANDs, working together with Him, you will bring blessing to other people as they see God at work in your life. Some years ago, I had a much loved cat called Jock and one day he went out and didn't come back. I looked and looked BUT I never found him.

Two weeks later my neighbour came round in tears. Her cat was missing. I was still trying to get over my own cat, let alone help someone else but through the disappearance of both cats, my neighbour came round AND God gave me a wonderful friend.

My new friend started to come to church and one day the Holy Spirit was moving in power and my friend began to shake. "What's happening to me?" she asked. "Oh, it's only the Holy Spirit," I said. "Don't worry."

Two days later, she rang me. "Margaret, I've got to get saved," she said. "As soon as possible."

"Margaret, it's urgent."

"What's so urgent?" I asked.

"The Holy Spirit. It's following me everywhere!" she replied. "Perhaps if I get saved, it'll leave me alone!"

"Perhaps He will," I replied. "Then again..."

My friend began her relationship with God that day.

I moved on from my BUT...AND God gave me a very good friend THEN blessing was free to come to other people.

So that's what God does. In the life of all those Bible characters. In the life of this woman at the well...in my life and in your life.

Sometimes He throws us a "curved ball". That's a baseball term. Everyone loves a straight pitch but a skilled pitcher can throw the ball so it travels on a curve. It's not something any baseball player wants to receive. And us neither...

When Kevin and I first got married we bought a house down the road from my parents and settled down to live an ordinary family life BUT then my mum died.

We decided we wanted to have some children and started to make plans for those children...BUT no children came.

We lived round the corner from friends and family and I had it all planned out BUT God called us to live our life hundreds of miles away from that place.

From time to time, a BUT happens and all our own plans fall into disarray.

What I have to ask myself is, "Will I be defined by the BUT or do I let it go and move forward with what God is doing?"

Wear your Badge with Pride

I began by mentioning a song and as the songwriter portrays, there are things in life that we can all say, both good and bad, "...I never expected that!"

A Badge of Promise

But there is something that God has given you and I that that songwriter didn't have. And that something is a *promise*.

Romans 8:28 says,

> *That's why we can be so sure that every detail in our lives of love for God is worked into something good.*

We can keep that promise hidden in a box or we can hold it up high. It's a badge of assurance that we can wear, and whatever happens we know that, *"...all things work together for good"*.

Wearing your badge doesn't mean you understand it! Wearing your badge doesn't mean you would have chosen it! But wearing your badge does mean that you acknowledge that HE IS GOD...and HE IS GOOD and you're moving on, with Him by your side.

And you can be sure that if you belong to Him, if you have committed your life to Him that whatever happens, ALL those things will work together for good in some way for you.

....

Consider:

1. Do you need to let go of some BUTs? If so which ones?

2. Do you need to recognise some ANDs already received and open your hands to some more? What are they?

3. Do you need to pick up that promise in Romans 8 and wear that badge of promise for all to see?

4. Why not talk to God about that now?

5

Time to Escape

He said, "Go call your husband and then come back." "I have no husband," she said. "That's nicely put: 'I have no husband.' You've had five husbands, and the man you're living with now isn't even your husband. You spoke the truth there, sure enough."

John 4:16-18

Let's look again at that part of our story when Jesus makes the difficult request. The two had been sitting by the well talking together when Jesus suddenly said to her, "Go and call your husband and then come back."

Jesus knew that there was something hindering her. He knew that she was still in darkness. He had talked about living water but she asked for it so she would never get thirsty again and never have to come to the well again. So she still did not understand fully that He was not talking about earthly water. She had a hindrance here which was revealed. Jesus knew that He must gently lead her to the thing that was destroying her life.

It was a huge request that Jesus made when He said, "Go and call your husband and then come back."

How did she feel? She knew the situation she was living in. The conversation was going so well and now this man was asking to see her husband?

I was trying to imagine how she felt when He asked her that. Did she feel ashamed? Embarrassed? Alone? Guilty? Defensive? Did she feel fearful?

I think she probably felt all of those but one of those six emotions has so much tied up with it because it isn't an emotion dealing with the present but it is more often than not, about the future.

Ashamed, embarrassed, alone, guilty and *defensive* are generally feelings of immediacy or of the past but the last one, *fearful,* can involve present events but it can also often be all about the future.

And in that moment, she was no doubt fearful of many things. She would be fearful of being lectured to, put down, considered worthless by Him, disapproved of, ignored and possibly a lot worse.

Jesus had *done* none of those things. He had simply given her an instruction but her FEAR would at that moment be taking her into the realm of the future. In other words a fear of the unknown!

Fear of the Unknown

A while ago, I went on a course with school called Music Technology. Now I have no problems with the 'music' bit. But it was the 'technology' angle that worried me! You see, when I first started teaching, a desktop was the top of a desk, 'phishing' was something that your dad did in a river and a 'byte' was something you took out of a sandwich. But times have changed and in a moment of madness, I signed up for the Music Technology course. My expertise to date was

was answering emails, finding websites and maybe downloading from itunes on a very good day.

I eventually found the right part of the building and on picking up my badge from the reception desk, I was shown the wireless code which was displayed on the desk. Searching for an illusive pen and paper from my bag, I turn to see someone simply whip out their iPhone and photograph the code. Why didn't I think of that?

I then visited the display area and became hijacked into a conversation with a computer sales rep about the perils of cookies (which to me at the time were American biscuits) random access memories and a universal serial buses!

Eventually, I managed to escape and head for the lecture room. We were then given the Twitter address and Facebook page so we could interact with the lectures (some hope I thought) and I trotted off to my seminar. I sat at the back as far away as possible from the lecturer.

We were instructed to get out our iPad or laptops – and switch them on. When mine came on first time, I was very encouraged!

"Now," the lecturer began, "please check that firstly, you have the correct IOS, secondly, click on the SSID, thirdly make sure your USB is plugged in and then finally, open up the PDF." It could have been in Japanese for all I understood!

The worst part was when I realised half way through the morning, that within the app we were using, at any point the lecturer could show our work on her screen at the front as an example.

Being as I'd only written x's every time we were asked to enter something onto our computer, I sat in fear and trembling in case she chose mine and all everybody would see was a page full of kisses! I was totally in fear about the unknown.

On the way home I got lost in a snow storm but that was nothing to surviving a day on the course for Music Technology!

People can have fear of many different things: flying, public speaking, heights, the dark, intimacy, death, failure, rejection, spiders, commitment, loss of freedom, pain, disappointment, loneliness, rejection and much more. Look on the internet and you will find hundreds of fears and phobias.

So often it's *what will happen* that we are fearful of. Fear of the unknown.

It's not the 'height' that bothers you, it's the fear, "Will I fall down there?" It's not the 'spider', it's the worry, "Will it come near me?" It's not 'commitment', it's the concern, "Will I get trapped?" It's the unknown information: what will happen in the future?

We can get an attack of the *What ifs* and the *What ifs* then become prison bars. *What if* the test results are bad? *What if* he leaves me? *What if* she marries that man? *What if* it all goes wrong?

I read on the internet recently that someone once said that FEAR should stand for **F**ace **E**verything **A**nd **R**ise. But so often in our lives it is **F**orget **E**verything **A**nd **R**un!

Stories In Your Mind

It's amazing how similar fears are to *stories:*

Fears have *characters* just like stories (when I see the doctor, what will he say?).

Fears have *plots* (what if I lose my job, and then I can't pay my bills and then I lose the house and then I have to live on the streets?).

Time to Escape

Fears have very powerful *mind imagery* just like stories.

Fears have *suspense* (what will happen next...?) just like stories.

Fears use *mental time travel* just like stories can (what if I stand up there and I can't remember what to say?).

And fears have a *sequence.* One thing always leads to another (someone you love goes for tests and by the end of the thought you can be picking the funeral hymns!).

AND the most important similarity of all is that *fears have us as the authors* (with a little help from somebody who is definitely not our friend!).

What are the anxieties which write stories in your mind?

Fear of loneliness?

Fear of failure?

Fear of illness?

Fear of looking stupid?

Fear of what others might think?

Fear of losing someone close to you?

Fear of being rejected?

Fears for your children?

Fears of old age?

Our book *Across the Brook* tells my husband's story. Kevin was born into a house of fear with his dad having two nervous breakdowns. Kevin developed a stutter and found incredible difficulty speaking at all, let alone in public. When he became a Christian, he began to be asked to give his testimony and speak in public, and after refusing many times he made a decision to *"say yes and worry later"* and the rest, as they say, is history. He spends his life now doing the very thing that was impossible! It's amazing what God can do when we say *yes*!

"Do not fear" is the most repeated command in the Bible. Out of all the commands, that one is mentioned the most. That's because God knows there are many things which we could be afraid of. But just to say to someone, "The Bible says *'don't fear'*" usually doesn't help them. In fact, it makes them feel guilty too!

So how do we deal with this huge issue of FEAR when it attacks our mind?

I want to suggest four things that can help us:

- Forget
- End
- Accept
- Recognise

1. FORGET what has gone before

(Deal with the PAST)

I had a great life until I got married! I was carefree, in love and planning my future my way. Then suddenly, everything went wrong. My mum died suddenly, my dad was seriously ill, my appendix burst resulting in peritonitis, our six year old nephew was killed in a road accident and throughout all of this, we were unsuccessfully trying to have a family. Life suddenly became very unsafe.

This left me with an enormous fear and anxiety about illness and death. I had my fear and the past had caused it. I wanted to forget it, but I couldn't. It took me, over a period of time, to bring these events in prayer to the cross, to repent for any resentment against God, to forgive any people involved and to repent for my attitude towards them and then allow the light of God's presence to wash over those hurts.

When I recognised the cause and I acknowledged it, when I brought it out of darkness and into the light and recognised the false beliefs it had left me with, it began to lose its power in me. While ever I kept denying it, I couldn't get rid of it. Once I found a place to be honest with God, I was able to move on from those bad experiences – into the future.

2. END the mind time travel

(Deal with the FUTURE)

Put an end to the imagination! Thoughts would fill my mind. What if I die like my mum? What if something happens to Kevin? What if there's a road accident? What if I've not got a baby by the time I'm 40? What will happen next?

For most of us, the problem is fear of the unknown. What if? What if? What if? You see, fear doesn't exist anywhere except in the mind. Fear is not real. The only place it can exist is in our thoughts.

When I was young, I was an avid *Dr Who* fan. Watching William Hartnell, the white haired old doctor fight the Daleks at 5.15pm every Saturday night, I would be ready to get into the Tardis and time travel to wherever the doctor chose to take me. And many of us still do that! Mentally we time travel, and so often we are so ready to get in that mind Tardis and go to wherever, not the doctor, but wherever the enemy chooses to take us. In our thoughts we can be in yesterday, tomorrow, anywhere at any time. We cross bridges that are not even built.

3. ACCEPT where you are

(Deal with the PRESENT)

It was when I began to acknowledge how things really were that they began to change.

If I was truthful with myself, I was disturbed. Yet I was saying all the right things and claiming all the right promises. So often, we say, "I shouldn't feel like that", "I am a wicked person". And it doesn't help us, it just covers our feelings of fear with guilt.

Start from where you're at. Be honest with God. Talk about it. God knows where you are. Denying it won't hide it from Him. Give yourself permission to be there and recognise it's just part of the process of moving on. Cast all your cares on Him. It's great to claim the promises of God but it's always healthy to be honest with yourself and with the Lord.

4. RECOGNISE the spiritual dimension

(Deal with the UNSEEN)

I then attempted to turn my fear into a weapon. To fight back. I used that fear. Everytime it hit, I decided to thank God for something I *did* have, something I *could* do. I allowed it to turn me to prayer and towards a relationship with God I didn't know before. I allowed it to force me into His arms.

Why not turn that panic into intercession? Use the sword of the Spirit which is the Word of God and speak out those promises of God? Even allow it to develop a relationship with someone new as you seek someone out to pray with you about the problem? Turn what the enemy means for harm into good.

Allow all things to work together for good and let some good come out of it.

Jesus said... *"go and find your husband and bring him here..."*

PAUSE...

There was a moment when she had a choice. It was a time window. Did she retreat? Disappear? Give in to that fear of the consequences? Did she forget everything and run?

Or did she respond? Did she face everything and rise? What did she do?

"Oh, so you're a prophet! Well tell me this..."

She launched into a discussion about Jews and Samaritans and the temple and worship, the result of which was that she discovered something that would set her heart on fire. Some commentators say she was evading the issue, and changing the subject. Some say that she was saying "you've seen my life, you're a prophet and you are spot on". But whatever the reason, she ended by saying, *"I don't know about all that, but I do know the Messiah is coming and when he arrives we'll get the whole story."*

And then Jesus speaks three wonderful words...

"I am He."

And He speaks that to you and I two thousand years on...

Who can help my son?

I AM HE

Who can heal my heart?

I AM HE

Who will walk with me through this problem?

I AM HE

He Changes Things

"Perfect love casts out all fear." And when fear comes as a flood to put out that fire within you, the Son comes and the heat of that sun evaporates that flood and allows the fire to burn bright again.

When God's love touches our heart, He changes us on the inside and displaces the fear with a love that is so much stronger and broader and deeper and all encompassing than any fear could ever be.

I was driving through a village in Lancashire recently and sandbags were at the doors, huge puddles were covering the road and the river was almost level with the bank. Two weeks later, I drove through the same place and the roads were dry, the river was down and the sandbags were gone. Had the village moved? Had a lorry with a suction pipe sucked up all the water? No, the sun had come out and the heat of that sun had dried up all the flooded ground. For some of you, there are floods of fear around your heart. Why don't you allow the Son of God to shine on you today and evaporate that fear away? Jesus says to you "I am He" and He can do all things.

Could it be that your heart is flooded with fear? Maybe it's whenever you meet a certain situation or maybe it's continual. I'm asking you to bring your fear to the foot of His cross. To come before God and allow the light and heat of His presence to beat down on your life and evaporate the flood of fear from your heart. I'm asking the Son to shine on you right now.

....

Consider:

1. Do you need to begin to take the steps above to FORGET and move on?

2. Do you need to END the mental time travel?

3. Do you need to identify and ACCEPT where you are just now?

4. Do you need to RECOGNISE the attacks and fight back?

The Well and The Woman

6

Knowing God as Father

"Believe me, woman, the time is coming when you Samaritans will worship the Father neither here at this mountain nor there in Jerusalem."

John 4:21

A while back I found an old photograph. It's a photo of myself and my father, who died many years ago, standing on a bridge. It's taken from the bank and shows us standing side by side, leaning on the bridge looking into the water. It's not a good photo, the top of my dad's head is cut off and it's not a good view of either of us. But I love that photo because when I see it, it reminds me of a great father and it's a picture that captures a moment which sums up my relationship with my dad.

My dad was a great dad. When I was small, he would tuck me into bed and tell me stories of his time in the army such as when the soldiers moved the tent and the sergeant major fell in the cesspit, and I would listen to the same stories again and again. He was fun and would dab my nose with paint as I walked past him, painting the wall (much to my mother's displeasure), and he would make us laugh.

At his instigation, he and I would sit tapping our cutlery on our plates singing "why are we waiting?" as we waited for dinner to be brought in by my mum. I have many good memories of my dad in my childhood.

But we are all not so fortunate. Kevin's experience was totally different and, due to nervous illness, his dad was often angry or depressed. Life's circumstances initially caused this but his father's problems, responses and choices made life very difficult as Kevin was growing up.

You, yourself may say, "Yes, I had a great father" or you may say, "My experience was not good" or even, "My father was not there at all". We all come from a whole range of experiences.

Our Invisible Father

But there was a point for all of us, who are Christians, when we became aware of an invisible world and we connected into a relationship with an invisible God and we began a journey in that world.

And we see this God in Revelation when John writes:

> Then I looked, and, oh – a door open into Heaven. The trumpet-voice, the first voice in my vision, called out, "Ascend and enter. I'll show you what happens next".
>
> I was caught up at once in deep worship and, oh! – a Throne set in Heaven with One Seated on the Throne, (suffused in gem hues of amber and flame with a nimbus of emerald).
>
> Twenty-four thrones circled the Throne, with Twenty-four Elders seated, white-robed, gold-crowned. Lightning flash and thunder crash

pulsed from the Throne. Seven fire-blazing torches fronted the Throne (these are the Sevenfold Spirit of God).

Before the Throne it was like a clear crystal sea. Prowling around the Throne were Four Animals, (all eyes. Eyes to look ahead, eyes to look behind. The first Animal like a lion, the second like an ox, the third with a human face, the fourth like an eagle in flight. The Four Animals were winged, each with six wings. They were all eyes, seeing around and within).

And they chanted night and day, never taking a break,

"Holy, holy, holy

Is God our Master, Sovereign-Strong,

The Was, The Is, The Coming."

Every time the Animals gave glory and honour and thanks to the One Seated on the Throne (– the age-after-age Living One–) the Twenty-four Elders would fall prostrate before the One Seated on the Throne. They worshiped the age-after-age Living One. They threw their crowns at the foot of the Throne..."

Revelation 4:1-10

So here we see a God who created all things, has great strength, and is all powerful. There are verses throughout the Word of God which describe Him as a *consuming fire, King of Kings* and *Lord of Lords* and many other majestic titles which place Him high over anything or anyone who has ever existed.

But God knew that it was difficult for us to relate to Him in this context because we have no human experience to relate to this kind of invisible God. And so He decided to speak a language we could understand. If you want to communicate a message, you have to speak in the right language.

He knew that we hadn't had a *mighty God* before, but most people had a father and in making this revelation, He was speaking in language that we could easily understand. He was saying, "I am your Father, your giver of life".

Our Earthly Father

But by definition in these days, the name *father* can sometimes be a difficult role for us to appreciate and positively identify with.

Today twenty five percent of all families with children in Britain have no fathers. And of those that do, many of them are good ones but some of them are not good fathers.

The Bible says that it was God's design that it would take a male and a female to make a baby and in God's ideal plan, a male and a female to bring one up. But in these days, the role of *father* has become blurred or in some cases nonexistent. So there is a need more than ever before, for God to reveal Himself as a Father to this fatherless generation.

And for you and I, life is not always ideal and although we all have a mother and a father, we wouldn't exist if we didn't, some of you maybe had an absent father. Maybe your father was absent physically, through death or divorce or even work. Maybe your father was absent mentally, and their mind, it seemed was always elsewhere. Maybe your father was absent emotionally and they seemed unable to connect with you on an emotional level at all.

Our Example From Above

But the great news is that when you are a child of God, God can make that up.

And whether or not you or I had examples from our fathers on earth, we do have an example from our Father in heaven, when He came to earth in His bodily form as Jesus, and God in the form of His Son was living and letting us watch Him do it.

He said,

> *To see me is to see the Father. So how can you ask, Where is the Father?*

John 14:9

He said,

> *Believe me: I am in my Father and my Father is in me.*

John 14:11

He said,

> *That's how the Father will be seen for who He is in the Son.*

John 14:14

The Message Bible gives a great description of Jesus,

> *No one has ever seen God. This one-of-a-kind God expression, who exists at the very heart of the Father, has made him plain as day.*

John 1:18

In the Old Testament we read of God mentioned as Father only seven times, but once Jesus came along we see God mentioned as Father a huge one hundred and fifty times. And not only did Jesus talk about God the Father much more, He also completely exploded the stereotype of God. More than anyone else, Jesus is the one who introduced us to the Father and encouraged us to live in the presence of the Father.

Our Life in the Shade

Why is knowing God's fathering presence in our lives, so important?

When a little baby arrives on the earth it has needs. Physically it needs food, clothing and shelter, mentally it needs stimulation and education and emotionally it needs love, affection and security, and we have these needs too.

And whatever our background, God, as our Father can provide all the things we need, for He created us.

We clearly know this truth, but sometimes there are things which cloud the truth, for example, tragedies happen and we grow up thinking God is not a loving father. Or we are taught in church that God is angry or judgemental and we grow up seeing Him as just that.

Fathers are imperfect and in some cases we grow up entirely unable to imagine a Heavenly Father such as God being full of love and positive attributes.

Many things can cloud the truth that God is a Father with a heart of love for His children. The truth is there, but clouds cover the truth.

In Scotland we have lots of cloudy days, sometimes for weeks when we don't see the sun. A couple of years ago, in mid summer, there was a headline in the newspaper, which read *"It's still up there folks..."* because it was so long since we had seen the sun. But in real life on cloudy days, we know the sun is still there. It never enters our head that the sun might have gone. We know that if we go up in an aeroplane it will be shining up there. Down here, the clouds might cover the sun but *the clouds can't stop it from shining!*

And so often our experience of our Father can cause unbelief in our lives. We know in our head He loves us but if our father never showed it or tragedy struck our lives or people taught us that God is an angry God, we find it very difficult to experience that promised love from our Father in heaven because there are clouds of unbelief that get in the way.

We know in our head that He delights in us but if our father never seemed to delight in us much, we can find it very hard to believe that our Father in heaven does. We live in the shade! There are clouds of unbelief that get in the way. The unbelief clouds our experience of God, just as the rain clouds out the sun but those clouds don't change the facts! The clouds of rain can't stop the sun from shining and the clouds of unbelief can't stop our God from loving!

Our Altered Perspective

God wants to make up to us, all we have lacked in our human experience. If no one said *"I love you"* or *"I'm proud of you"*, He wants to make it up to you. And this, for all of us, is a lifelong process.

A while back, I heard a good friend preach the following:

> "You are a winner! You may not feel like a winner at times but YOU are a winner. On that day you were conceived, you won. When those millions of cells rushed towards that ovum, you had a one in five hundred million chance of getting there first. And you won! And your Father in Heaven planned that you would win."

And what did He feel when He saw you beginning to grow in the womb? You were special to God long before you were born. What did He feel when you were about to be born? He felt excited that you were going to live on earth and that you were going to hear about Him and find a relationship with Him and begin that journey in the world He had created.

Experiencing God as Father, more and more as time goes on, causes us to grow up.

When I was very young, my father and I used to play a game. At mealtimes, we would sit at the table and my dad would place the things I liked best on the edge of his plate. After a minute he would look away and I would carefully remove the kidney or the strawberry or the radish from the plate and eat it. Then he would look at the plate and say, "Oh no, Roger the mouse has been here again!" And we would play this game over and over again.

As I grew from three to four to five to six Roger often came to join us at our mealtimes. But sadly, one day Roger the mouse didn't come any more. One evening my Dad put my favourite food on the edge of his plate and I didn't take it. The little mouse didn't come. Why? *Because I had grown up.* And you know, that wasn't a sad day. It was a happy day because that's what my parents wanted. They didn't want me to stay a mental three year old all my life. (I assure you Kevin and I don't play that game every meal time!) They wanted to watch me thrive and grow and succeed in confidence and ability and they wanted to see me fly! My dad wanted me to pass on to others all he had tried to pour into me. And your dad in heaven wants exactly the same for you! This changes your life.

A little while ago, it was reported in the papers that the Archbishop of Canterbury had discovered that the man he had believed to be his earthly father, wasn't actually his biological father. It was splashed over all the papers as everyone waited for his response to this devastating news. When it came, he simply described his revelation of God as his Father then he said, "I knew on that day, that God was my Heavenly Father and nothing can touch me after that." End of story.

And as we allow God to shower down His Father's love on our life, we begin to grow up, we change our perspective and we pass on all He has put into us, to those He has called us to.

And although your earthly father may or may not have done so, your Heavenly Father sees the aspiring hero in you, His child. Whoever you are, wherever you are from. He is your cheerleader!

Do you need to explore this more in the next few days or weeks or months? Because the Father's Heart experience is something that changes and deepens depending on where you are in your life and He will have different things to shower on you now, than a year ago.

Fifteen years ago we lived in an apartment just outside Glasgow which stood on a hill and looked down over a large golf course then onto a beautiful park. Beyond the park was the city of Glasgow then behind that, the Campsie Fells and Kilpatrick Hills. What a view to wake to every morning. In the ten years I lived there, I never got tired of gazing at the view because it was always different. Whatever the weather, snowy, sunny, cloudy or rain, there were different nuances to see each time.

Our Incredible Benefits

And with God it's the same. In *Great Thoughts from a Little Dog*, we spend a month meditating on the different attributes of our Father God. Different nuances of the same relationship.

Listed below are those same benefits of knowing God as Father:

- You are provided for
- You are delighted in
- You are safe
- You are forgiven
- You are helped
- You are comforted
- You are energised
- You are nourished
- You are enlightened
- You are trained
- You are an heir
- You are delivered
- You are healed
- You are lifted
- You are watched over
- You are guided
- You are given joy
- You are spoken to
- You are given health
- You are tested
- You are given victory
- You are satisfied

- You are given peace
- You are drawn close
- You are set apart
- You are heard
- You are blessed
- You are answered
- You are shown faithfulness
- You are strengthened
- You are redeemed

He has different things to reveal to you now than He did last year. Why? Because your needs are different.

I have been a Primary School teacher for many years and just now, one day a week, I teach music throughout every age range. At 9am, Primary 4 arrive, at 10am Primary 6 arrive and so on, throughout the whole day. What I teach to Primary 1 is different to Primary 7. It's the same subject but I have *different things to reveal to them*. Why? Because their need and their understanding is different. And God does the same depending on where we are in our life, growth and situation.

Why not read the book of John and search for more of the Father? Or look at the different ways Father God revealed Himself in your life and then write your own story?

Why not allow more of those clouds to be removed so the bright sunlight can shine on your life?

....

Some people have a very positive earthly photo in their mind like mine. Some haven't. But whatever you see, good or bad, you do have a heavenly photo of a Father God who leans on a bridge with you, who relates to you, to talks to you, who listens to you and who loves you.

Are you going to pick it up today? A picture which you will keep close to your heart because it captures a moment which sums up your relationship with your Father God?

Remember, you're a winner! You won that race because He planned you to, because He has a plan for you and His Father's heart pouring into your life can make this 'life journey' a great one.

You may be sitting here reading and you know there are clouds above you which are blocking out the sun. Maybe your cloud of unbelief is caused by an uncaring or absent father or maybe it is caused by something that happened and you ceased to really believe God was a loving Father or maybe you were brought up on an angry God? Whatever caused these clouds, it doesn't matter now because the wind of the Holy Spirit wants to blow the clouds away today.

Maybe you had a photo of your loving God, but you've dropped it. Somewhere along the way, like mine, it got lost. Or maybe you've never picked it up?

Just because you have no earthly photo, doesn't disqualify you from a heavenly one. It's there and it captures a moment which sums up your relationship with your Heavenly Father.

Why don't you pick it up right now?

Now turn back to the thirty one benefits of knowing God, consider them one by one and spend some quality time with your Father.

7

In Spirit and in Truth

*It's who you are and the way you live that count before God.
Your worship must engage your spirit in the pursuit of truth.
That's the kind of people the Father is out looking for: those
who are simply and honestly themselves before him in their
worship. God is sheer being itself – Spirit. Those who
worship him must do it out of their very being, their spirits,
their true selves, in adoration.*

John 4:23-24

If today, I was to take you to our home and you were to walk
into our sitting room, you would see hanging over our
fireplace, a large framed photograph. And it is a photo of a
huge, red, sandstone rock called 'Uluru'. This rock is over
two miles long and over one mile wide and it descends
underground for a mile and a half. It is hard to take in how
enormous it is.

When we were on holiday in Australia, we decided to go to
visit this major tourist attraction. So we flew to Alice Springs,
hired a car, studied a map book, pointed the car in the right
direction and travelled for 280 miles across the outback until
we came to stand before this rock.

The Well and The Woman

We went on the journey and we followed the book and as a result we acquired something new in our lives.

We now have a picture on our wall that is not just a picture but every time we look at it, our minds are filled with so many memories of our time in Sydney, Melbourne, Adelaide, Darwin, Perth and Alice Springs.

We bought something away with us from that experience that adds to our life.

And it is God's agenda, that when we go to a conference, listen to a podcast or read a book, it becomes part of our spiritual journey.

We are all on a lifelong spiritual journey. For some of us, maybe we are still on that journey towards God to discover if He is real or not. For many others, we have found God as a personal friend and after finding Him, we journey through life with Him by our side.

And this God who journeys with us, is a God of deeper, higher, further and wider!

We read in the Psalms:

> *If I climb to the sky, you're there!*
> *If I go underground, you're there!*
> *If I flew on morning's wings*
> *to the far western horizon,*
> *You'd find me in a minute –*
> *you're already there waiting!*
> *Then I said to myself, "Oh, he even sees me in the dark!"*
> *At night I'm immersed in the light!*

Psalm 139:8-11

We read in Romans:

> *Do you think anyone is going to be able to drive a wedge between us and Christ's love for us? There is no way! Not trouble, not hard times, not hatred, not hunger, not homelessness, not bullying threats, not backstabbing, not even the worst sins listed in Scripture.*

Romans 8:35

We read in Ephesians:

> *Reach out and experience the breadth! (God's love) Test its length! Plumb the depths! Rise to the heights! Live full lives, full in the fullness of God.*

Ephesians 3:18b-19

There is no boundary that God CANNOT get across to meet us, and there is no place God is NOT. In the highest heavens, in the deepest oceans, in the earliest morning, in the farthest seas, in the latest nights, and sometimes, aren't those just the exact places we find Him?

In other words it's actually in the sacrifice, that He appears the brightest. Climbing that bit higher up, swimming that bit deeper, rising that bit earlier, waiting up that bit later. Because when we do these things, we often see a different world to the one we see every day.

If you've ever been up a mountain pass and looked across the mountain tops. How did you feel? If you've ever been to the depths of the countryside and looked up on a clear night, how did you feel?

When we go on holiday, we often watch people learning to dive and I know that once they descend underwater they are experiencing a whole new world that I don't even know exists. Early in the morning there is a deep stillness around and people say you can see the world and your world in a new way. Late at night, really late when everything is still, that's often where we can meet God.

It's often in making the sacrifice that God responds to our action.

Jesus told the woman at the well that there was a time coming when believers would worship Him in Spirit and in Truth. And we are in that time. God calls us today to worship Him and to connect with Him in Spirit and in Truth. As we worship in Spirit and in Truth, then He will give us the right eyes to see our world in a new way. As we soak in the Holy Spirit and the truth of God's Word, He will help us find a place in our thinking, for events that happen in our life.

How do we begin to worship Him in Spirit and in Truth?

1. Be still with God's Word

As you read right now, you have chosen to stop your activity and to turn your mind to God and His Word as you read the Bible verses within this book.

You cease to work, to look after the kids, to do housework or whatever you usually do at this time and you make a choice to be here, to read, to open your own Bible and to be STILL.

Psalm 46:10a says:

Be still and know that I am God. (NKJ)

Psalm 37:7a says:

Quiet down before God,
be prayerful before him.

Psalm 23:2-3a says:

You have bedded me down in lush meadows,

In Spirit and in Truth

you find me quiet pools to drink from.
True to your word,
you let me catch my breath.

The other week it was the thirty fifth anniversary of my mum's death and I was thinking on that day that if she were to walk in the kitchen at that moment, all the things I would show her.

I would say, "Mum, I don't have to wait while dinner cooks in the oven any longer, I put it in the microwave."

"Mum, I don't have to wait weeks for a reply to a letter I send abroad. I send it, and it comes back through this computer in just a couple of minutes."

"Mum, I don't have to wait to use the phone to ring my friend in Derby, I have my own little personal phone and there are little messages that come through from her many times a day."

"Mum, I don't have to wait two weeks while the librarian orders a book from another library to get me the information I need, it is on this thing called *Google,* twenty-four hours a day, seven days a week."

"I don't have to wait till the bank opens on Monday, I can go to the cash machine or flash a plastic card at a machine on a shop counter any time I buy something."

"I don't have to wait till the shop opens tomorrow. I can go to an all-night supermarket and buy exactly what I need."

My mother would be amazed I'm sure at all these things.

But we know, that for everything we have gained, one thing we have lost, is the ability to wait. We are not used to doing it. The ability to just think, to be still and as Christians to let our minds soak in the truth of God's Word.

Sometimes it's just good to step out of our instant world, to find a new space. And to be still. To allow God's truth to calm us, to inspire us, to correct us, to strengthen us and to cleanse us.

It's a **mind** thing and it's a **God** thing.

We need to fill our mind with the truth of the Word of God and as those truths fill our mind we don't have to bring them to life. They are already alive and active, sharper than any two edged sword!

Take time: To think. To worship. To dwell. To soak, in that truth that is alive.

2. Be filled with God's Spirit

Jesus promised that God's Spirit would come to us.

Ephesians 5:18b says,

> *Drink the Spirit of God, huge draughts of him.*

1 Corinthians 12:13b says,

> *Each of us is now a part of his resurrection body, refreshed and sustained at one fountain – his Spirit – where we all come to drink.*

Matthew 3:11b says,

> *The main character in this drama – compared to him I'm a mere stagehand – will ignite the kingdom life within you, a fire within you, the Holy Spirit within you, changing you from the inside out.*

1 Corinthians 6:19a says,

> *Or didn't you realise that your body is a sacred place, the place of the Holy Spirit?*

In Spirit and in Truth

Isaiah 44:3b says,

> *I will pour my Spirit into your descendants and my*
> *blessing on your children.*

John 20:22 says,

> *Then he took a deep breath and breathed into*
> *them. "Receive the Holy Spirit," he said.*

John 14:17b says,

> *But you know him already because he has been*
> *staying with you, and will even be in you!*

1 Corinthians 3:16 says,

> *You realise, don't you, that you are the temple of*
> *God, and God himself is present in you?*

We fill our stomachs with food, we fill our car with petrol, we fill our pocket with money, so we can use those things, for energy to live, for fuel to travel, for cash to spend. We wouldn't invite guests for a meal with no food. We wouldn't drive our car with no petrol. We wouldn't buy possessions with no money and yet, so often, why do I expect to be able to feel the Holy Spirit's touch on what I say, and I do, and I plan when I haven't bothered to fill up with Him? We need to say regularly, "Here is my heart Lord. I have made some space for you. Please fill me up."

Space is a vital part of life. If you listen to a piece of music, the thing that makes the music effective, is the silence. If you read a book, the thing that makes the story live for you are the things the author *doesn't* say, the spaces where you can use your own imagination. The space creates a longing or a drawing of you into the story. Something happens in that space! When you watch a film, it's what the director doesn't say that draws you, if he told you everything about the storyline then it gets boring. It's when someone hides a paper in a drawer but you don't know why, when someone's hidden from sight just watching, but you don't know why. It's the spaces in the information that draw you in. Something happens in that space.

When we come before Almighty God, the thing that makes the connection for us are the things we're *not* doing, the things we're *not* saying. Something happens in that space!

It's a **heart** thing. It's a **God** thing.

We need to fill our heart with the presence of the Spirit of God.

We truly need to fill our **mind** with the **truth** of the Word of God and fill our **heart** with the **presence** of the Spirit of God. We then connect with God in truth *and* in Spirit

3. Be Envisioned with God's Light

Ephesians 1:17-18a says,

> *I ask – ask the God of our Master, Jesus Christ, the God of glory – to make you intelligent and discerning in knowing him personally, your eyes focused and clear, so that you can see exactly what it is he is calling you to do.*

2 Samuel 22:29 says,

> *Suddenly, God, your light floods my path,*
> *God drives out the darkness.*

Psalms 18:28 says,

> *Suddenly, God, you floodlight my life;*
> *I'm blazing with glory, God's glory!*

Psalms 19:7-8 says,

> *The revelation of God is whole*

and pulls our lives together.
The signposts of God are clear
and point out the right road.
The life-maps of God are right,
showing the way to joy.
The directions of God are plain
and easy on the eyes.

Proverbs 6:23 says,

For sound advice is a beacon,
good teaching is a light,
moral discipline is a life path.

As we worship in Spirit and in Truth, as we spend time allowing the Holy Spirit to fill our heart and allowing the truth of God's Word to fill our mind, then He will give us the right eyes to see our world in a new way. In His way. Our vision next week, next month, next year will be clear.

As we soak in the Holy Spirit, and we marinate in the truth of God's Word, then this will help us find a place in our thinking, for events and problems that happen in our lives, so those situations do not cloud our vision.

As we make space and as we let the Spirit and the Word interact within that space, then He will cause something to happen.

I know that when I am full of the Holy Spirit then God gives me the eyes to see my world differently. He just does.

Everywhere is 'God filled' if you bring the right eyes to it. And whenever we find ourselves soaking in the Spirit, worshipping in the Spirit, praying in the Spirit, listening to the Spirit, being full of the Holy Spirit, He gives us the right eyes to truly see our life and our situation.

At the same time, nowhere is 'God filled' unless you bring the right eyes to it. You can be on a beach of blue sea, blue sky and palm trees but if you are full of sadness then you could be in a prison. But in the same way, you can sit in a prison and if you are full of the Holy Spirit and feel His peace then you could be somewhere beautiful.

I have some words written in an old Bible which I have read many times throughout my life,

> *Two men looked out from prison bars.*
> *One saw mud, the other saw stars.*

God has given us a land to possess. There will be things that come against you getting to that place of fixing your mind on the truth and filling your heart with His Spirit; problems, busyness, apathy, distractions. But there is a place for you. When we allow God to lead us to this place of His presence, there is everything you need.

The Rock That Never Moves

When I look up above our fireplace at the picture of Uluru then it fills my mind not only with memories of a great time but it refreshes me for the day ahead and the challenges I have to face.

When we went to see Uluru there were hundreds of people sitting watching, and we sat for two hours or so and just watched it. It was constantly changing because as the sun moved across the sky, the shadows the sun created kept highlighting different facets of its shape.

And as we spend time with the rock in whom we can take refuge then we will see that although our God never changes, although He is *"the same yesterday, today and forever"*, He is whatever we need Him to be at any moment in our lives and those shadows in our lives, when they come will throw up amazing views of our God.

As today you look to a place of space that is yours, soaked in the Holy Spirit and dedicated to the truth of the Word of God, it will give you eyes to see your life on God's big screen and as the Word and the Spirit come together, you will be envisioned for tomorrow.

There *is* a place for you.

Consider:

Maybe you feel like you've been travelling through the outback. For one reason or another, it feels like your source of the Holy Spirit has dried up. The reason could be a problem, busyness, stress, a distraction in your life or complacency and as you've been reading, you've been scanning the horizon and you've caught a glimpse of that rock.

1. Why not tell Him those things right now and thank Him as the living water floods over your life once again.

2. Be still. Be filled. Be envisioned right now.

8

The Water Pot

Just then his disciples came back. They were shocked. They couldn't believe he was talking with that kind of a woman. No one said what they were all thinking, but their faces showed it.

The woman took the hint and left. In her "confusion" she left her water pot. Back in the village she told the people, "Come see a man who knew all about the things I did, who knows me inside and out. Do you think this could be the Messiah?" And they went out to see for themselves.

John 4:27-30

We see here that Jesus is deep in conversation with this woman, the disciples return from going to get some food and then the woman leaves the scene, but on leaving, she leaves her water pot behind. The Bible doesn't actually say why she left her water pot. Just that she did.

Why do you think she left that water pot?

It could be that she was so impacted by Jesus' words that she totally forgot her errand to the well. It could be that she was in a hurry to let Jesus eat and not bother Him further. It could be that she left the pot for Jesus and the disciples to have drink. Or it could be that she left it so she could come back, and talk to Jesus again.

We don't know why she left it.

But I want to explore three further reasons why she could have left the water that she had collected and apply them to our lives today.

When I was eight years old, I wandered into a small wooden hut, I heard about Jesus and invited Him into my life. If you are a Christian, there was a time, maybe a moment or maybe a longer period of time, when you came to the realisation that you needed Him as a friend. You needed Him to forgive your sins and to fill you with His Holy Spirit so you could live daily with His presence in you and around you.

So for most of us who read this book, we come to this place filled with the living water that He spoke to the woman about. But sometimes we leak! Problems, stress, busyness and many other life events cause our water pot to become dry.

Why **did** the woman lose her water pot that day?

Past Memories

> *He said, "Go call your husband and then come back." "I have no husband," she said. "That's nicely put: 'I have no husband.' You've had five husbands, and the man you're living with now isn't even your husband. You spoke the truth there, sure enough."*

> John 4:16-18

That wasn't what she was expecting when she set off for the well that morning or even when this stranger began the conversation! But by what Jesus said to her, we know that she'd had quite a past!

We all have a past, a present and a future. Life happens and it's a very rare person who goes through the whole of life with no trauma along the way.

But such is our society that we seem to give great emphasis to physical pain but little emphasis to emotional pain. When Princes William and Harry began to talk of the impact of their mother's tragic death on their lives, they received a very mixed reaction from the public. Some loved it and some hated them, as members of the Royal Family, being so transparent.

In our culture we practice physical first aid but rarely emotional first aid. We deal with physical injuries but mostly leave psychological injuries to fade into the past.

And we get to feel that these weaknesses in our personality or our emotional make up, disqualify us from ever doing anything really great for Him. Brokenness, however, is not just an idea of God to make our life difficult, but brokenness is God's *requirement* for maximum usefulness. In other words, it's the cracks in you that allow the Holy Spirit to flow out. It's as you share how God helped you through traumas, that others think, he's human, she's not perfect, if they can do it, I can do it.

As people watch you walk through tragic circumstances and they see Him get you through to the other side, without knowing it, they see the power of God at work in some very difficult times and they think *I want that*. It's as He breaks us and puts us back together again that He can flow through those cracks and His light can shine.

So rather than disqualifying you from an effective life, as you let Him heal those pains, those things actually qualify you for greater service and use to His glory.

Present Relationships

Just then his disciples came back. They were shocked. They couldn't believe he was talking with that kind of a woman. No one said what they were all thinking, but their faces showed it. The woman took the hint and left.

John 4:27-30

This reason is not in the past. It's very much in the present.

We see that the woman was very comfortable speaking with Jesus, in fact she took a full part in the conversation. She even continued the conversation when Jesus began to bring up the past. But she was not comfortable with the reaction of His friends. It was other people which were causing her a problem.

And you and I live in a world full of people. Some live thousands of miles away, and some live so close to us that we form relationships with them, and within the range of our relationships, we have healthy ones and sometimes difficult ones. Good ones and bad ones.

Is it because of current relationships that you so often lose that blessing He pours out on you? You go to church on a Sunday and by Monday, the blessing of the day has drained away. Do you need Him to imprint in your heart that it doesn't matter what others think or do? All that matters really is what He thinks and does, and He will help you keep that blessing.

Get objective – step back, look out for those words, comments or actions that cause you to lose that blessing. I had a friend and after a while, I noticed that each time I met her, I came away feeling disturbed. So I got objective and began to recognise little comments she made which were due to her own issues but were aimed at making me feel bad. Once I recognised them, I started to count them, and recognising what was happening helped me stay objective and keep my own sense of well-being. Try it!

Just as Jesus showed interest in this woman, as she was, your God is interested in you, just where and as you are. To Him, it doesn't matter what other people think. It matters what He thinks. And He thinks you are special.

Future Assignments

Back in the village she told the people, "Come see a man who knew all about the things I did, who knows me inside and out. Do you think this could be the Messiah?" And they went out to see for themselves.

John 4:28-30

The woman rushed off and wanted to tell as many people as she could and,

...many of the Samaritans from that village committed themselves to him because of the woman's witness.

John 4:39

Because of the result, we know that she did the right thing but I ask myself, how often do I rush off from the presence of Jesus, into the FUTURE for the wrong reason?

How often do future tasks and assignments cause me to prematurely leave His presence?

Speed is a fashion of our times. We are constantly racing against the clock. We have speed reading, speed walking and speed dating. We don't wait in a queue, we self-serve at the supermarket to get through quicker. We hurry through life. We feel that if we are not using time, we are wasting it.

I teach piano and have many children come to the house each week. Some of them go swimming, dancing, canoeing or running and they are literally rushing into piano from some club and then running out to another.

It seems that even children are going faster and faster!

There are now movements rising up such as the *'slow food movement'* which is dedicated to taking time to cook food, having time to eat food properly and enjoy it, and replenish relationships at the same time.

In a similar way, in the *'slow cities movement'* city leaders dedicate their city to a slower pace, providing green parks, seating and benches for reflection and areas of nature for people to walk in.

For many people, *'doing nothing'* has gone. Yet it's something that puts our thoughts in order, it's healthy but it's so hard to do.

Here are the regrets heard most often by palliative care staff at one hospital:

> 1. I wish I'd had the courage to live a life true to myself, not the life others expected of me.
>
> 2. I wish I hadn't worked so hard.
>
> 3. I wish I'd had the courage to express my feelings.
>
> 4. I wish I had stayed in touch with my friends.
>
> 5. I wish that I had let myself be happier.

No one has ever said on their death bed, "I wish I'd spent more time at work", "I wish I'd been busier". It's worth thinking about.

....

The Water Pot

We have no idea whether the woman lost her water because of the past, remembering those mistakes and hurts of past days or whether it was because of the present and the reaction of the disciples was all too much. Or whether it was because of the future and there were things to do and places to go. But one thing is sure, she left her water supply at the well.

Consider:

1. Are there things in the past which you feel disqualify you from His blessing? What are these things? What did you learn from these things? Why not ask God to cover these things with His love and then recognise them as your qualification and training for your usefulness to Him?

2. Are there problems or relationships in the present which steal your blessings? What are they? Who are they? Recognise these for what they are. Step back and get objective. When the enemy uses these things against you, recognise them for what they are and keep walking.

3. Are you always rushing to the next thing on your list? Why not plan now to make some space. When will it be? For how long? Plan it and do it just once and before you leave, plan it again. And do it.

9

Naturally Supernatural

Many of the Samaritans from that village committed themselves to him because of the woman's witness: "He knew all about the things I did. He knows me inside and out." They asked him to stay on, so Jesus stayed two days. A lot more people entrusted their lives to him when they heard what he had to say. They said to the woman, "We're no longer taking this on your say so. We've heard it for ourselves and know it for sure. He's the Saviour of the World!" After the two days he left for Galilee.

John 4:39-43

What a shock! The woman was suddenly transported from the back to the front, from the tail to the head. Amazingly, the people in the village asked Jesus to stay longer with them and He stayed with these people for two whole days. That in itself was a miracle! Samaritans would never invite a Jew to stay in their home. As a result, a lot more people entrusted their lives to Jesus when they heard what He had to say.

This woman's life changed. She took what she had and gave it away.

The Well and The Woman

I'm sure there wasn't a lot that she had which people wanted but they wanted this. She changed lives. She became naturally supernatural. Her heart had caught fire and she went round setting other people on fire.

Not long ago, I read a story on the internet:

Tim was at university and it was his very last day. A girl walked up to him and told him that three years before, it had been her very first day at Uni. She felt so nervous that, as her parents were helping her unpack, she burst into tears and explained to them that she didn't think she could go through with it. They assured her that she was only to say the word and they would take her back home.

She went on to tell Tim that at lunch time on that first day, she was standing in the dinner queue with her parents and she felt even worse. She was just about to tell them she wanted to go home when suddenly, she saw Tim over her mum's shoulder. He had just walked into the room, dressed in a silly hat with a bucket of lollipops in his arms. He started to walk along the line of diners and hand them out. When he got to the girl, she said, he stopped and looked at her. And then instead of giving her a lollipop, he gave it to the guy in front of her and said,

"You just have to give this lollipop to that incredibly beautiful woman standing right behind you." The guy in front of her looked very embarrassed and took the lollipop and handed it to the girl, embarrassed even to look at her.

"I don't know," said Tim. "Look at that! It's her first day away from home and she's already taking sweets from a stranger!"

Everyone around burst out into laughter.

"I knew at that moment, that something inside had changed and that everything would be OK," she continued. "I've never spoken to you before but I heard that today was your last day

and I wanted you to know, in that moment, you changed my life.

"Oh and also, by the way," she said, as she turned to go "Me and that guy who was in front of me, we want to invite you to our wedding in December!!"

Tim searched his memory. He had no memory of that at all. But simply by sharing what he had, that lollipop moment had changed her life.

Do you give lollipop moments? You see our life matters to others. We can be powerful in someone's life and not even know it. We can bring influence, just where we are. Just as the woman did. You can change stories!

Have you ever *received* a lollipop moment? I've had people that have given me lollipops. Jean Shepherd gave me a lollipop when in 1965 she asked me to come and join in and listen to the story. It changed my life. Jackie Clark and the team gave us a lollipop when they decided to take a chance on someone who'd never pastored a church before, and said come up and be the pastor in Glasgow. It changed our life. And I'm sure that you too have had your lollipop moments. The more you think about it, the more you'll find. People who have touched your life and maybe they don't even know it.

Are you prepared to give out *supernatural* lollipops?

Who are those people? Where are those people? To be Jesus to them and maybe you'll never know it!

But in order to do that we need the power of God to touch us.

It's great to experience God as loving father, as friend, as comforter. But it's also good to sometimes remember *who He is.*

The woman in our story gave out lollipops. She said, *"COME, SEE a MAN."*

That's exactly what we are called to do. We invite people to *"COME, SEE a MAN."*

1. Come...

Firstly, we invite people to come to a place where maybe they don't often come.

I clearly remember the first time I took my first dog to dog class. I had no idea where to find the place, where to park or by which door to enter. I didn't know when to pay, where to sit or which class to join. My dog spent most of his time either super shy, quivering under a chair or super friendly with his nose stuck up the bottom of the dog in front! I spent most of the class watching the amazing exploits of the dogs in front of me thinking *"my dog will never do that"*. I was so pleased I had walked him beforehand so no fear of you know what!

Then it was his turn, and when in fright he began to squat down, I knew what was coming next! I ran, grabbed him and with his tail firmly pressed under his bottom, ran out of the door! It was my first and last visit!

It's difficult, going where you've not been before!

But we ask people to approach, arrive, move towards, reach out to a place they don't know or don't feel is relevant to their life. For some people, inviting them to church is like someone asking you to come to the meeting for the *Over 40s Greengrocers' Annual General Meeting*. Or the *AGM for the Administrators of the Lions and Tigers Society*. Or the *First Retreat for the Second Cousins of Old Soldiers in the Boer War!*

For you and I, our relationship with God and our church attendance is living, and vital and a big part of our lives. But to someone who's never been, it seems irrelevant. They don't know that it's a place you can step out of your everyday life to get shade in the noonday sun. They don't know that it's a safe place you can go back to again and again whatever is happening in your circumstances; a place that you can be revived and refreshed in your spirit and face the week ahead under a spiritual covering and protection in the unseen world; a place that provides brothers and sisters that can stand with you in life whatever you face. When we are asking people to come – they don't understand all that. It's just you that they see.

2. See...

So we ask people to come where they don't come. And secondly, we ask people to see what they don't see. Those Samaritans couldn't see Jesus. Jesus was out by the well.

We have a good friend and a while back, his wife June was diagnosed with a short time to live. We heard the news and as soon as possible, went to see her. We sat in their lounge and listened.

"I'm 78 years old," she said. "I have had a great life and if God wants me home then I'm more than happy to go."

And over the next six months, we watched this couple who spent their lives teaching people to live well, start to teach people to die well.

"I feel like I'm waiting for a bus," she used to say so often, "to take me on to heaven, and I'm here at the bus stop ready." There was no fear, just a readiness – because she could very clearly see where she was headed.

One morning her consultant wasn't on duty and a colleague came to check on her. The doctor was very impacted by June and from then on, he came every morning before he began his operations, just to sit in the room with her. He wasn't a Christian. He couldn't yet see – but he knew that *she could*.

She was giving him lollipops!

And then one Sunday morning we received a text. It simply read, *"The bus arrived for June at 1.45am this morning. I am ok and resting in God's presence. No better place to be. Be blessed today."*

June could now see clearly what we see only darkly.

When people clearly see that you can see something they can't, they start to look. Stand in the street, point to the sky and try it!

3. A Man...

Come, see "A MAN" were the woman's words. She said, *"Come see a man"*, but she was yet to find out that He was so much more than a man. He was also her supernatural God.

And it's the *something supernatural* which draws people to come and draws people to see. Because He wasn't just a man. He was God.

And He isn't just a man in history. He is God in the here and now.

I want to share four pictures and I want you to use your imagination to see these real events. If you have quiet music available, use it now.

I want to introduce *ELOHIM* our all-powerful creator of the universe. Our amazing God who knows all, creates all, who is everywhere at all times.

Find a quiet place, read these words out loud, slowly and meaningfully and meditate on each one. Think about each word before you speak the next.

1. Think of Creation

Earth was a soup of nothingness, a bottomless emptiness, an inky blackness. God's Spirit brooded like a bird above the watery abyss.

God spoke: "Light" and light appeared.

Genesis 1:2-3

Imagine it...

CREATOR

AUTHOR

ORIGINATOR

INVENTOR

AWESOME GOD

OUR MAKER

He is creator of all things...

2. Think of His Position

Look around you. Everything you see is God's, the heavens above and beyond, the Earth, and everything in it.
God, your God, is the God of all gods, He's the Master of all masters, A God immense and powerful and awesome.

Deuteronomy 10:14,17

Imagine it...

AUTHORITY

PRE-EMINENT

KINGLY

OMNIPRESENT

ROYAL

OUR FATHER

He is Mighty God...

3. Think of His Coming

The sun will fade out,
moon cloud over,
stars fall out of the sky,
cosmic powers tremble.
And then, they will see the Son of Man enter in
grand style, his arrival filling the sky – no one will
miss it!

Mark 13:25-26

Imagine it...

MAJESTIC

OMNISCIENT

NOBLE

MAGNIFICENT

REGAL

AMAZING

He is all powerful...

4. Think of His Grandeur

There He is: Sky-Rider
Striding the ancient skies
Listen – he's calling in thunder

Naturally Supernatural

Rumbling, rolling thunder.
Call out Bravo to God, the high God of Israel.
His splendour and strength rise
Huge as thunderheads
A terrible beauty, O God
Streams from your sanctuary.

Psalms 68:33-35a

Imagine it...

        SUPREME

          PRE-EMINENT

            POWERFUL

              OMNIPOTENT

                MIGHTY

                  OUR STRENGTH

He is awesome...

You are Creator

You are Mighty God

You are Powerful

You are Awesome

And you are my God who touches my life.

And it is you, Creator, it is you, Mighty God, it is you, awesome Elohim, it is your power which reaches down to touch me in this moment...

....

141

The Well and The Woman

Now be still and experience the presence of God.

God *is* comforter, healer, equippcr, and deliverer. But God is God, and from Genesis through to Revelation, we see His majesty and His supernatural dealings with His children.

Let that supernatural power of God flow through you

right now…

If you have never begun your own relationship with Jesus, why not do that today by praying the prayer below:

Dear God,

Thank you that you are beginning to open my eyes to your world.

I want to say in this moment, here is my heart – I have made some space for you.

I am sorry for my wrong doing and I ask you to forgive my sin and change me from the inside out.

Let your light flood my life and ignite the kingdom life within me.

I ask you to be the rock that never moves in my life, from this day on.

Amen

In the Eastern Christian tradition, the woman at the well is celebrated as a saint of renown. As told in John 4:28-30 and John 4:39-42, she spread the news of her experience with Jesus and through her many people came to know Him personally for themselves.

In this Eastern Christian tradition, she is believed to have preached the gospel fearlessly even though she was instructed to practise her faith in secret. She is believed to have brought many, many people to know Jesus, so much so that she was eventually brought before high authorities to answer for her faith and was tortured and died as a martyr. In some countries there is an annual remembrance of her life and all she accomplished.

The Orthodox Christian Faith, http://orthodoxchristian.info

Other books by Margaret Peat:

The White Elephant

Eleven real life stories about people who dealt with issues such as loss, inferiority, and forgiveness. A devotional book to work through your own issues as you read.

The Seagull

Eleven more stories about real people dealing with life topics such as putting God in a box, the power of words, the effect of sowing and reaping. A devotional book for you.

Dear Sally

Presented in the form of letters which Margaret sent to a close friend, this book works through eleven powerful life principles to weave into your own life and experience.

Great Thoughts from a Little Dog

If you don't like dogs, don't buy this book! A 31 day devotional for dog lovers based on the benefits of knowing God as Father. Enjoy a dog parable a day!

Across the Brook

Kevin and Margaret share their individual stories as they journeyed along their first 25 years of life. This book shows how anyone can discover a perfect Father's love.

The Journey

A spiritual journey into God's presence borne out of messages Margaret has ministered over the years. It is packed with wisdom, insight, and a good dose of humour!

Family at War

Sharing the story which emerged from Margaret's own family research, she shares the challenges they faced and gives practical and deep spiritual insights to build up, encourage and inspire.

For orders please contact: KMPeat@aol.com